Strange, But True

STRANGE, BUT TRUE.

LIFE AND ADVENTURES

OF

CAPTAIN THOMAS CRAPO

AND WIFE.

NEW BEDFORD:

CAPT. THOMAS CRAPO, PUBLISHER.

1893.

PREFACE.

The voyage of Captain Thomas Crapo and his wife in
a dory boat from New Bedford, Massachusetts, to England, although several years ago, is as fresh in the memory
of the people as though it was but yesterday.

I did not see them or the boat when they sailed, but I
was anxious to get the daily papers, in order to find out
if they were reported, and was more than pleased to see
that every time they were reported they were both well
and in good spirits.

And at last the papers announced the arrival of the
captain and his plucky wife at Penzance, England.

People did not think so much about the captain making
the attempt as they did the idea of taking his wife along.
And as the voyage was ended without any serious dis-
asters the newspapers of every country loudly applauded
them.

Since it was reported that the attempt was to be made,
I was very anxious to see the hero, but never did, to my
knowledge, until about five or six years ago, when I in
company with my wife attended one of the churches on a
Sunday evening. When near the close of the evening
services the pastor extended an invitation to every one
present who would like to testify for Jesus. Several
responded and gave their testimony, when presently a
gentleman directly in front of me arose and made a few
remarks. After concluding his speech the pastor spoke
in this manner, as near as I can recall it: Thank God,

after years of trials and tribulations on the briny deep, and crossing the Atlantic Ocean in a small dory, Captain Crapo at last acknowledges his Superior, and now stands before the whole world a living witness for Jesus Christ. Praise the Lord.

I was all attention at once; the one I had longed most to see was before me, and I could scarcely keep my eyes from him. As I had sailed the ocean myself I could readily foresee some of the dangers they would have to face in that little boat, and his wife being with him, when there was scarcely room for one and turn around, made the matter worse, as they would naturally encounter gales, when the captain would find it all he could do to look after the boat, to say nothing of his wife.

After their arrival they had a little book printed about the voyage, which they sold for five cents, and everyone seemed to want them. I got one through a friend of mine, and eagerly devoured its contents.

A short time ago I was introduced to the captain by his wife, whose acquaintance I had made nearly two years before, and I found him a modest, unassuming man, and not addicted to bragging about his exploits.

In talking with him on several occasions I made up my mind that no adventures had been written that could equal the personal experience of the captain of more than thirty years at sea, and I proposed the idea of publishing his adventures to the world.

After carefully considering the matter he at last consented to do so, as many people had advised him the same a great many times before.

But, says Captain Crapo, the people of to-day are looking for something romantic, that never really existed, and would probably think my book too tame, as I will not have anything in it but truths whether it sells or not; and therefore, kind reader, you can be assured that every word enclosed between the covers of this book about Captain Crapo and his wife are facts, and no fairy tale to mislead.

So with the kind permission of our friends everywhere we will begin our story as told by the captain himself, as correctly as he can recall the facts; many of minor importance, no doubt, have passed from his memory long ago, but those coupled with his experience written in this book he will probably remember as long as he lives.

THE AUTHOR.

CAPTAIN THOMAS CRAPO.

THE CAPTAIN'S STORY.

CHAPTER I.

I WAS born in the city of New Bedford, June 27th, 1842. My mother died when I was but eight years of age. I attended the public schools until I was about fourteen, when I ran away from home to go to sea. I had been desirous of becoming a sailor for a long time, but my father had always objected, so the only way for me to do was to run away from my home, which, as many others had done before, I saw no reason why I could not do the same.

The more I thought about it the more determined I was, and as the whaleship Marcia was nearly ready for sea I left my home and shipped aboard of her as cabin boy. The Marcia was commanded by Captain Billings, and we sailed from New Bedford on the 25th of August, 1857, bound for the North Pacific Ocean.

As the custom has always been, the crew was shipped on what is called a lay. I was to receive the two hundred and fifteenth, which meant that of every two hundred and fifteen barrels of oil caught by the ship one belonged to me, or the equivalent in money, and the bone in the same proportion. And as the outfitters, termed sharks, usually charge a hundred dollars for clothes that could be bought for twenty-five dollars at any clothing store, the sailors cannot justly claim anything from the ship until their bill, with interest, is paid. And the clothes they sell to the poor sailors as a general thing scarcely hold together until they get into deep water, and the tobacco that can be bought at any tobacco store for fifty cents, they charge the sailors one dollar per pound. ˙ Anything to rob the poor, misguided sailor, who, as soon as his money is gone, is off again on another voyage.

I was informed that my duties were to keep the cabin clean, wash dishes, black the captain's boots, and make myself generally useful.

Our crew numbered thirty-five all told, which was the usual complement for a whaleship that swung four boats.

Our crew consisted of captain, first, second, third and fourth mates, four boat steerers, cook, steward, cooper, carpenter and cabin boy, and twenty-one seamen, some of them able seamen, ordinary seamen, and the balance were` green hands making their first voyage.

As usual when a ship sails, relatives and friends of the crew accompany them down the bay, returning with the pilot on the pilot boat. The pilot while on board has full charge of the vessel, and remains on board until she is in deep water with plenty of sea room. The captain assumes command as soon as the pilot leaves. A large number went down with us and everything was bustle and commotion, and one could scarcely tell which of them had shipped for the voyage, as they were up and down the forecastle, and in fact around all parts of the ship; and dinner being served while they were on board, they partook of it with the rest, and many of them seemed to like the hardtack, as it is called.

At last our friends were called to accompany the pilot back to New Bedford. With handshaking and wishes of good luck they depart, and we proceeded on our long voyage. On seeing them depart, and knowing it would be four long years, if ever, before I should see any of them again, caused me to regret the step I had taken; but, alas!

it was too late. I was booked for four long years, and no way to do but grin and bear it.

While gazing longingly at the receding shores of my birth I was aroused from my gloomy thoughts by the captain, who, in a loud but pleasant voice, summoned all hands in the waist of the ship. Not knowing where it was, I followed the rest, and as they stopped in the center of the ship I did the same, concluding that to be the waist. After all hands had gathered there the captain stated very plainly to us that every one on board must obey the order given by the officers, and do their duty to the ship and themselves. He wished to see everything pleasant at all times, and if any trouble should arise to report promptly to him and he would attend to it; for, said he, we are as brothers while on this ship, and our main object is whale oil, and each and every one of you must keep a sharp lookout for the whales; and in order to remind you of it I will offer as a prize a quantity of tobacco to be given to the one that raises the first whale.

After he had finished talking, the officers proceeded to choose their boat's crews, each of the officers as they rank —first, second, third and fourth mates—choosing one at a time until they were supplied, those not chosen to act as ship-keepers while the boats were down for whales, or if anyone was sick or disabled to take their place in the boat.

Then each one is instructed what oar they are to pull and what other duties were expected of them.

The first mate's boat is called the larboard boat, the second mate's the waist, and the third mate's the bow boat; the fourth mate's is called the starboard or captain's boat, and is generally used by him when he wishes to go after whales himself, and is also used for gamming purposes.

What is meant by gamming is for vessels to meet in their travels across the ocean, when the captain of one will take

a crew and row or sail, as the case may be, over to the other
vessel, which brings the two captains together. The mate
of the ship visited takes a crew and goes back, which brings
both first mates together. The sailors are always on the
lookout for a gam, as many times they hear from home and
stories are told, songs sung, and a general good smoke all
around, and generally the cooks are ordered to get up a
special dinner or supper for all hands; sometimes in good
weather vessels will gam for several days.

The crews of the first and third mate's boats are called
the port or larboard watch, and those of the second and
fourth the starboard or captain's watch.

Having been assigned to watches, the port watch was
sent below, and the starboard watch remained on deck
making sail and coiling up rigging, as night was fast
approaching. At half-past six the watch below had their
supper ready to relieve the watch then on deck at seven
o'clock. I watched the steward get the sidelights ready
to be put up in the rigging, one green and the other red,
where they remain until daylight. When the clock in the
cabin indicated seven o'clock, the boat steerer that was
steering struck the bell hanging just behind him eight
times, when the watch below came on deck and those on
deck went below, to remain until called at eleven o'clock.

On taking charge of the deck an able seaman took the
wheel, the one relieved giving him the course to steer, and
another was posted on the topgallant forecastle to keep
a sharp lookout ahead, the watch being in charge of the
first and third mates, who walked the quarter deck, and,
as is generally the case, the crew are called aft quite often
by the command of haul main braces, in order to turn
her sails to the wind.

At nine o'clock the man at the wheel strikes the bell
four times, when another takes his place, the one relieved

instructing the one relieving him what course to steer, and another of the watch relieves the lookout by taking his place.

At eleven o'clock the wheelman strikes eight bells, when the third mate usually calls the second and fourth officers, one of the crew calling the watch from below. When they are all on deck the watch relieved goes below to sleep until three o'clock, when they again muster on deck, as watchers are on deck four hours and below the same.

Before morning I was not only homesick, but seasick as well, and if I could only got on shore I don't think anything would ever tempt me to try it again. Being cabin boy I slept in the cabin, which was far superior to sleeping in the forecastle, where the sailors are always cramped for room, and seasickness in such a packed-up place must be awful.

I did not have to stand watch, but every time that bell rung for the first few nights I heard it.

The next day the officers and boat steerers got out the whale lines, and began to splice them in order to have them long enough to suit. Then the harpoons and lances were ground, the sailors turning the grindstone. The long and short handled spades are ground, and we were ready for whales, each boat steerer supplying his boat with four or five irons and lances ready for use in case they are needed.

The lookout rings were also put up, two at the foremast, two at the main and two at the mizzenmast. The officers and boat steerers keep lookout at the main and the foremast hands at the fore and mizzen. The captain also generally stands masthead several times a day.

Masthead lookout is relieved at four and eight bells through the day, and during the dog-watch from four to six o'clock in the afternoon; both watches are on deck at once, and are generally kept busy by washing the deck.

A boat's crew consists of an officer, boat steerer, one man at the stroke or after oar, one at the tub, who, when a whale is struck, must immediately dash water onto the line to keep it from getting on fire, a midship and bow oarsman, making a list of six all told.

A whaleboat is supplied with the following articles: one large tub of line; one small tub of short line; four or five harpoons; three or four lances; a lantern keg with a antern, matches and hard-tack in it, to be opened only when fast to a whale all night or out of sight of the ship; a bomb gun and bombs to shoot into a whale and explode inside; a mast and sails; paddles; a keg of water to drink, also a small piggin to drink out of for a dipper; a hatchet; short spade; sheath knife and a drague, to make fast to a whale if possible when a boat gets stove; and several other small things, which, coupled with the oars and six men, fill the little boat, about twenty-eight feet long, pretty full.

The paddles play quite a prominent part in a whaleboat, as in case of light winds the crew sit on the gunwale and paddle as hard as possible after the whales; but it must be done without a noise, as whales are easily startled, when off they will go like the wind.

During the first five or six days I remained below most of the time, being too sick to be about, as anyone that has ever been seasick would know, and how I longed to be at home; and as I said to myself many and many times, if I was there I would stay and be contented. Yet every one on board was kind to me and cheered me all they knew how, but that was not what I wanted; I wanted to go home to New Bedford, but as I began to feel better I was more contented, only the water and victuals did not suit me, yet I fared better than the sailors.

To those that have not been to sea I will say that fresh water put into new casks in hot weather is not much of a luxury at any time. After it has been in the cask a few days it gets ropy and stringy, and is by no means palatable, not even after it settles and works clear; it still has that flat, nasty taste, and is enough to turn some people's stomachs.

And the grub, as sailors say, that is still worse. Just imagine for a moment the cook taking a piece of salt meat from the cask, salted with saltpeter and soaking it all night in salt water to freshen it, and then boil it in salt water, and after boiling skims the grease that rises to the top to make scouse, as it is called, for the crew. Scouse is made in this way: put a quantity of hard-tack into a canvas bag and break it up with a hammer and put it to soak in water over night; then for breakfast warm up the grease and cut up some of the meat and mix it all together; surely to see it you would think it rather uninviting to make a dinner of, yet sailors as a rule get it to eat every morning, and the same mixture baked, which don't improve it any, for supper. When you hear sailors speaking about lob scouse this is the mixture they mean, and dandyfunk is nearly the same, with molasses put in to tone it up, as extra. In order to get a change the sailors catch albicores and skipjacks, which are usually very plentiful, as they follow a ship for months.

Meal cakes, more commonly called Johnny cakes, are very good for breakfast, but sailors don't think so, as the way they get them is the same as the farmers give it to their chickens, merely mixed up in warm water, and full of lumps as large as a bird's egg. This is to be eaten with molasses, which is furnished in small quantities, and codfish balls, the fish usually being so rancid as to be unfit to eat, as it will not hold together; but we get it pounded up in water, and as potatoes are usually quite plenty you can add them to suit yourself. There is no necessity of having a salt shaker as everything will be found salt enough.

At dinner you get baked beans, which is generally quite palatable, and one from each watch divides them, so each will receive his share. And the next day for dinner you get soft-tack, a sailor's name for white bread, which is seldom soft, but very hard and heavy, and many times very sour to the taste; should you offer one to a common tramp I do not believe he would accept it.

Plum duff is a Sunday dish, and the plums are usually dried apples, and is the best dish on board of a whale ship, especially if it is made good; but many times the owners ship very poor cooks, and that, of course, means poor food; but if any fault is found the captain usually calls your attention to the fact that there is plenty hard-tack in the main hold, and you can eat that, which is not much satisfaction at best, but one must do it or go hungry. By breaking up hard-tack in water sweetened with molasses and a few drops of vinegar, called swanky, you can relish quite a breakfast for a change, and sailors usually get very fat on it.

As each man washes his own dishes after eating, the cook is not bothered with them; and as they usually consist of a small pan and tablespoon and quart tin cup, with sometimes a knife and fork, it does not take them long, as they generally pour in a little water and rub it around and wipe it and it is all done. The sailors are not bothered with butter dishes, as they do not get the butter, but I had some in the cabin, as there is where they do get it, also in the steerage among the boat steerers.

On account of such poor food the sailors many times exchange clothing for better bread and butter or anything good with the boat steerers.

I do not know what the tea is made of that is served for supper, but the bucket the sailors get it in will be about a quarter full of large leaves, and look as though they had been gathered in an apple orchard in the fall of the year; yet the tea was better than clear water. The coffee served for breakfast is made of roasted barley, and is quite good.

But to proceed with my story. About twenty days from home we sighted the Azores Islands, more commonly called the Western Islands, inhabited by Portuguese. We ran in at Fayal, one of the largest, but did not anchor, as our stay was to be short; the captain did not deem it advisable, as it is considerable trouble to haul the cable from the locker amidships and put the necessary turns around the windlass and shackle it to the anchor, as a large quantity of slack is needed to anchor in safety, besides the water is one hundred and twenty feet deep and upwards, which takes a large quantity of chain in order to give the vessel a good scope for holding fast; so we shortened sail and let her drift around, called laying off and on.

On arriving the captain lowered with a boat's crew and went ashore for letters, fresh meat, potatoes, onions, yams and cabbages, and so forth, the crew remaining in the boat until his return. He also shipped three Portuguese for the balance of the voyage.

After the supplies were put on board we squared away, bound south. I watched those islands as long as I could see them, as it seemed good to me to see land again, as I had not yet become reconciled to my position, but they soon disappeared from view as we continued on. While in the latitude of the equator (termed the line) a large school of sperm whales was sighted. The captain immediately called to the officer in charge of the deck at the time to call all hands and get the boats ready for lower-ing; the watch below are awakened, jump into their clothes as quick as possible and get on deck. The first thing to be done is to put the tub of line (which is usually kept on a rest on the rail close to the boat made for that purpose) into the boat and stand ready to climb down the side of the ship to drop into the boat as soon as she strikes the water. The mate in his place in the stern and the boat steerer in the bow are lowered in her to cast off the falls as she settles in the water. The first mate starts lowering when the rest follow, when the falls are cast off the boat drops astern of the ship, when the mast is stripped and the sail set, and off we go after the whales. I stood at the rail watching the boats all the time, wishing I was in one of them, as I was very anxious to see a whale.

No sooner had the sails been set than the sailors took their paddles and each boat strove for the lead, and excite-ment ran high, each crew doing their best to beat their companions.

As soon as the boats are lowered the captain goes up to the foremast head and signals to the boats with a flag kept for that purpose. When the whales are up he hoists the flag and takes it down when they sound. When the whales are ahead of the ship the flying jib is hauled down; when on the bow the clew of the fore topgallant sail is hauled up; when on the beam the mainsail is hauled up, and when on the quarter the head of the spanker is hauled in, and when astern the whole spanker is brailed up; so by keeping an eye on the ship the occupants of the boats can keep run of the school.

The cooper stands at the main topmast and hoists an-other colored flag, when a boat makes fast, so the other boats will know, and be on the lookout in case assistance is needed, as many times a boat is kicked to pieces, especially sperm whaling, as a sperm whale is a fighter, and as he has teeth in his lower jaw (being the only whale that has teeth) he many times makes good use of them by biting anything he can get hold of. Many times they will settle in the water with their head up straight, and snap their jaws together in a fit of rage, which would snap a man's head or leg off in a jiffy, should he be unfortunate enough to get near it. Many times a boat is stove, leaving the crew to look out for themselves for hours, or until the ship can get to them, as the other boats are supposed to pursue the school as long as there is any show of getting a whale.

Everything went well until one of the boats drew along-side of a good sized whale, and the boat steerer took his stand with his harpoon poised ready to dart. As the boat drew up in the position that suited him he darted, and as luck seemed against him, his iron either fell short or went over the whale, which so frightened him and all the others that they made off with the speed of the wind. So the boats returned to the ship, the crew very much put out with the boat steerer for not making fast.

Whales usually swim along in groups like a line of soldiers, and the boat steerer always picks out the fattest and largest one, and in order to get him he must go between the flukes of two of them, which he must be very careful in doing, as when struck the whale raises his flukes high in the air and brings them down with a bang, intending to crush his slayer, and should both do so at once he would be in a rather uncomfortable position, as they would prob-ably swamp the boat if they did not strike it; or, as has been done, turn upon the boat and smash it to pieces, causing broken limbs and loss of life.

We again, after hoisting up the boats, continued south, nothing occurring worthy of mention until we arrived off

River Platte, when a heavy gale sprung up, which tossed us about like a chip. I did not feel very comfortable, as I expected we would go to pieces or be tipped over in the heavy seas which looked like mountains rolling towards us, and the ship rolled so and took on so much water, you could almost swim on deck, and I could hardly keep my feet, but thank Heaven it did not last very long, and I began to feel better, yet wondering in my own mind how a ship could stand such thumping, rolling and pitching. Those are the times a man with a cool head and good judgment is needed to save the ship from destruction, the loss of many occurring on account of the captain not being competent to do so, as many are promoted to the captaincy through favor more than experience, but Captain Billings was competent and knew what he was about, and I made up my mind to brave it out without any more fear.

After the gale abated and the seas quieted down a little, we cruised around for a few days but did not see any whales; so again sailed south, and in rounding Cape Horn the weather was terrible, the seas rolling mountains high, and the wind howling through the rigging.' I cannot describe it as I would, but as many times vessels are driven back and try for weeks for a favorable time to round it, my readers can form a little idea what it must be. But, though tossed about like a cockle shell for hours, we at last arrived in smoother water on the other side. We then squared away for the island of Mocha, on the coast of Chili in South America.

On arriving at Mocha we lay off and on as before at Fayal, the captain again going ashore for letters and provisions. When out of sight of the boat three of the boat's crew deserted. When the captain returned to the boat he was informed of the fact, when he again went ashore and offered a reward for their capture. The boat then returned to the ship, when the sailors told us about the men running away. After the captain had informed the officers of the desertion he sailed a short distance from the island, to make the deserters think he was going out to sea (deserters generally put for the mountains and remain hidden until the ship sails, when they come down among the natives), when about nine o'clock in the evening signal fires on shore announced the capture of the deserters. The first mate, with a picked crew, at once started for the shore, and soon returned with the runaways.

Runaways are generally punished by losing their watch below in the daytime for a period of time fixed by the captain, and only an allowance of hard-tack, and a stated quantity of water to drink, during the time.

We then squared away for Talcahuna, about three days' sail away. We saw plenty of whales, but the weather was such as to render it impossible to get them, so it was deemed advisable not to lower the boats.

On arriving at Talcahuna the cable was hauled from the locker amidship and rove around the windlass, and when shackled to the anchor was ready to drop into the sea in order to hold the ship against the force of wind and water. When in a satisfactory distance from the land the anchor was let go, when the vessel soon came to a standstill; then the sails were furled, rigging coiled up, while the captain went on shore for letters and supplies as before. After the supplies were put on board, and the ship put in shape, the crew was given liberty on shore, the starboard watch being the first to go, the captain giving each one one dollar and ten cents each day. Each watch had three days on shore. I do not know how much the boat steerers got, but I suppose about five dollars each day.

During our stay ten of our crew deserted. The captain again offered a reward for their capture. We then hove up anchor and put to sea, and on our return, a few days afterward, we found only one had been caught; the others were not so easily fooled, probably sure the ship would be back after them in a few days. So I did not see them again, as we squared away for the Galapagos Islands.

The barque Peru, of Nantucket, being in port for water and provisions, we sailed in company. When off the islands we sighted whales, the boats were got ready for lowering, and on account of so many of the crew deserting I was told to go in the third mate's boat, which I was more than pleased to do, as I was very anxious to see a whale close to.

And fortune favored our boat, as we soon drew alongside of one. I watched closely every move made by the boat steerer, as everything now depended upon him. As we drew closer to him the boat steerer stood up and braced his knee in the bow chock (a place sawed out for that purpose), then placed two harpoons in a crotched stick, fitted to hold them handy to reach, and as the boat got close to him he darted first one and then the other, the irons striking the whale just forward of his hump, and quickly sank to the sockets in the thick blubber. As the irons struck him he raised his flukes high in the air and brought them down with a bang which nearly swamped us, and it was lucky for us it didn't strike the boat, as it would have smashed it into pieces. He then started to run, and how we flew through the water; the water fairly boiled along the sides of the boat. I never rode so fast in my life before. He kept up his mad pace for a period of about ten minutes, when he slowed up. The third mate then exchanged places with the boat steerer (as the mate always does the killing), and ordered us to pull in the line which draws the boat up to the whale. And great care must be taken not to get in the coils, as the whale is liable

to take a fresh start at any time, when woe to any one who
gets afoul of it. We hauled close up to him as he lay
quite still, and the third mate proceeded to lance him, and
soon had him spouting volumes of thick blood, when we
drew away from him and let him have his flurry, which
was of short duration, when he rolled over on his side, fin
up, dead. We then drew up alongside of him, when the
officer cut a hole in his flukes and made the boat fast to
him, at the same time signalling the ship with a small flag
carried for that purpose, when the ship bore down and
made him fast with what is called a fluke chain run
through a hose pipe forward and around his flukes; it is
then made fast to a bit and we have him secure. Our
boat was then hoisted up and we were again on board.
We then made preparations to cut him in. A stage for
doing so is swung across the gangway in the waist, the
heavy falls made fast around the mainmast head, then the
turns are put around the windlass and all is ready for
cutting him in. The officers take long-handled spades
and cut the thick blubber, the crew heaving at the windlass, and as they heave it rolls the whale over and over so
the officers can cut it off; the large strips as they are hove
in are called blanket pieces. A boat steerer then is
lowered into the whale by a rope under his arms to reeve
head needle, so the head can be made fast and severed
from the body, which usually sinks as soon as it is stripped
of the blubber. The head of a sperm whale is hoisted on
deck unless it is a very large one, when it is lashed alongside. As the best oil is found in the head great care is
exercised in saving it, but many times they sink and are
lost.

It is surprising to see how quick the sharks will gather
around a dead whale, and while the boat steerer is overboard the officers are kept busy trying to keep them away

by cutting them with the long-handled spades, as they are very ravenous.

After we had completed cutting the whale in, we began to cut him up into what is called horse pieces, which are then put through a mincing machine, which scarps it similar to the pork in a pot of beans.

The pots were then got ready for use by filling them about two-thirds full of the case oil from the head (supposed to be the brains of the whale), which is sometimes bailed out of the head in buckets; then the fires are lighted, an officer being in charge of the boiling. After the head is all tried out the horse pieces are put in, and when the oil is all out of them they are screened off and put into a scrap napper to use for fuel, some always being kept to start the fires with. As the pots fill up the oil is bailed into a copper tank, called the cooler, and as that fills up it is then bailed into casks prepared by the cooper. I eagerly watched all the process it went through as it was new business for me, and after it was all finished I heard it made about thirty-five barrels of oil; so you see that with the two hundred and fifteenth lay it did me no good, yet it was a good start.

We continued to cruise around for a period of ten or twelve days, but as no more whales were seen and in a calm the ship was drifting toward the shore, the captain ordered all the boats down to try to tow her away. We pulled hard all day until about four o'clock in the afternoon, when a light breeze sprung up, which gave us a lead off shore, when the boats were ordered back to the ship. After hoisting them up we trimmed the sails and away we went, clearing the land in safety.

As the breeze held on we headed for the Sandwich Islands, about twenty days' sail away, and after a pleasant run we ran in and anchored off the Island of Mahe, one of the group. After fresh water and provisions were put on board we were again given liberty of three days each. While there I asked permission of the captain to go forward before the mast, as it is called, with the sailors, which he permitted me to do, as he had shipped a Kanaka boy in my place.

I then considered myself a sailor at once. I moved my chest from the cabin into the forecastle, and then had to stand watch, my trick (as it is called) at the wheel and masthead with the rest of the sailors.

I was assigned to the port watch and the first mate's boat, and was to pull his stroke oar.

While anchored there many of us received letters from home, from relatives and friends, which to a sailor is a luxury, as it carries their minds back to their school days, and many little things are brought to mind, and to think they are still remembered though thousands of miles from home, ofttimes brings tears of gratitude to their eyes, and many of them are read over and over again. While out of port it is no uncommon thing to go below and find a sailor reading and pondering over a letter from a father, mother or sweetheart. And they are eagerly looked for as soon as the captain after going ashore returns, and the glad look leaps into their eyes when he calls aloud their name. Again, on the other hand, there are those that do not receive any, and while others do, you can almost picture their feelings by watching them; their heart seems to be held in a balance expecting to hear their name called when it could jump for joy, and as there are none for them they turn on their heel as though a heavy weight was hung to them.

Before leaving Mahe the captain shipped enough Kanakas to complete his crew on account of those deserting.

There were about fifty vessels at anchor in the harbor while we were there, mostly whalers in for water, provisions, and to give the sailors a run on shore, and as we met a great

many of them we had a good time. Our third mate, a
Portuguese named Lewis, was taken sick, and the captain
gave him his discharge, and shipped another man in his
place.

After the crew had all had their liberty of three days
each, we hove up anchor and started for Honolulu. Upon
our arrival the captain went on shore and sent a lighter
out to us to take the thirty-five barrels of oil to send home
to New Bedford. These so-called lighters are large boats
built on purpose to take casks of oil from one vessel to
another, or on shore, as many times vessels are in port
waiting for a cargo of oil, and it is very easy to lower into
a lighter and take it to them, when they hoist it on board
and away they go.

After discharging we started for Kodiak, on the coast of
Kamschatka, in the northwest part of Alaska.

We cruised in company with several other vessels about
three weeks, all the time being in sight of Mount St. Elias.
We saw whales several times, but owing to heavy weather
and they being to the windward we were unable to get any.

While cruising around a dead right whale was sighted.
We lowered for him and took him alongside, and while
cutting him in we found a harpoon in his blubber marked
Montezuma (all whalers mark the name of their vessel on
the harpoon, so if found, those finding it will know what
vessel had owned it, as they would be considered the owners
of the whale should they come across him), and he proved
quite a valuable find by stowing down about one hundred
and fifty barrels of oil and fifteen hundred pounds of bone,
without the trouble of chasing and killing him, which
might have proved disastrous to us, as he must have been
a tough one, on account of being struck already by the
Montezuma's crew and then lost. No one knows but
what he stove their boat to pieces, or killed or maimed

some of them.   But be that as it may, we had him now in casks safe from harming anyone.

After a few days of leisure we again sighted whales; the boats were again lowered and off we went, each boat working hard for the lead.   Our boat was again high hook, by fastening to a large cow whale, which ran so fast that we were soon out of sight of the ship; and as she continued to run it was out of the question to think of hauling line on her, and we were getting further and further away.   The mate deemed it advisable to cut the line and let her go, which he did.   After watching her for a few moments we turned about and started back in the direction the ship was in when we saw her last.   (I neglected to say that each of the officers carry a small compass in the boat, and if there are signs of being run out of sight of the ship, they note the direction she was in when last seen, and in a short time we could see her mastheads.)   We kept on.   When within three miles of her we ran across two monster whales.   We immediately gave chase, and succeeded in making fast to one of them.   After running a short distance he slowed up and we soon had our boat up close to him, when the mate began to lance him in good shape and soon had him spouting blood quite freely; when just as the mate was nearly ready to back off, the boat steerer, through carelessness in not dipping his steering oar properly, and a large wave coming just at the time, threw the boat on top of the whale and capsized us all on his back, and it is a miracle that any of us lived to tell the tale, as he could have lashed us all to pieces in a few seconds, especially maddened as he was by being struck with harpoons and lances; but strange to say he merely settled in the water leaving us afloat.   And owing to the water being so cool, and I had so many clothes on, I went under twice and was going down the third time, when one of the crew

reached out an oar to me, which I eagerly grasped with all
the strength I had left, and was pulled up on the bottom of
the boat where the others had clambered for safety. The
others seeing our predicament started for us and took us
to the ship, and then put for the whale, as the mate had
already given him his death wound before capsizing.
They had no trouble in securing him.

As soon as I got on board I hurriedly made a change of
clothing, the others following my example. It was nearly
daylight when we got him made fast alongside, but he
proved a good catch worthy of all the trouble we had, as
he was very large and fat. We had just about finished
cutting him in when a gale sprung up which lasted about
six days, which made it hard work to boil down, as the
ship rolled so we could only fill the pots about half full.
But we finished at last, and after cleaning up we found he
had stowed down about three hundred barrels of oil and
three thousand pounds of bone.

Whales were in sight all the time during the gale, but
it was no use to lower for them, because we could not get
them alongside providing we got one or more, so no
attempt was made.

After the gale abated we captured three large ones without anything occurring worthy of mention. After cutting
them in we cruised around about three weeks without seeing a spout of any kind.

Then the captain concluded to run into Cook's Inlet,
thinking he might find whales there. The inlet is very
large and dotted with a large number of small islands; the
tide runs very strong. We saw several whales, and struck
one but lost him. We then ran further in and anchored.
The mate with his boat crew (I being one) went ashore
on one of the islands. We went along a very narrow path,
in single file, for a distance of nearly two miles, when we

arrived in sight of four or five huts or shanties, which proved to be an Esquimaux fishing station. The shanties were built of logs and shingled with bushes scattered all over the roof. The sides were about four feet high, and the top went up to a peak like an ordinary house, the most noticeable feature being the inside. On entering one of them we found bare ground for floors and a fire built in the center, with the smoke going out through the door and between the logs. Inside were also found several mounds built for the children, at least we thought so, as each of them contained a child from four to eight years of age, and to stand a short distance away you could hardly tell whether it was a child or a dog's head sticking out. They seemed to enjoy the situation as well as we did. We traded hard bread with them for salmon, which are found in large quantities and of unusual size, many of them weighing twenty or more pounds. After getting a quantity of them we again returned to the vessel. While on the way back the wind began to blow quite hard, and by the time we got on board it was nearly a gale, which increased until it was a regular hurricane, the seas rolling mountains high. We tried to heave in the anchor, but as there was so much strain on it, it broke the windlass, which caused all the chain to run out of the locker, and all that held was where it was shackled around the main mast.

And it is a fact, yet many may doubt it, with our heaviest anchor down weighing about twenty-five hundred pounds and seven hundred and twenty feet of chain attached to it, we drifted seventy miles to the leeward. And as she was drifting toward a lee shore, the captain ordered the royal and topgallant yards and then the topgallant masts sent down, which was very dangerous work at such a time. This was done on account of their holding so much wind aloft. The next order was to reef the top-sails and set them. He then ordered the cable slipped, which meant the loss of the anchor and all the chain attached to it. But he was looking for the safety of the ship and crew, and would willingly sacrifice a large number of them if found necessary to do so, to ensure the safety of the vessel.

By slipping the cable as we did was the means of saving our lives and the ship as well, as she barely escaped the breakers. Had she once got into them it would have crushed her as quickly as you could a blown eggshell by stepping on it. After clearing the point we had plenty of sea room, and the captain ordered the vessel laid to, which was done, and she rode out the balance of the gale admirably, after which we had better weather.

As it was now nearing the close of the season of 1858, the captain concluded to make for the Sandwich Islands. About four days before our arrival we sighted a school of sperm whales. The boats were lowered, and each of the four succeeded in capturing one. We took them alongside, and cut them in, when we again had plenty of work, as it is a case of little sleep and plenty of work while trying out whale. The crew generally get about six hours' sleep in twenty-four, until the blubber is all tried out. After cutting them in we proceeded again on our course, and soon arrived at Mahe, and for fully twenty-four hours after anchoring we were engaged in trying out, the four stowing down about one hundred and thirty barrels. We then hauled alongside of the merchant ship Yorick, of New Haven, Conn., and put all our oil and bone on board of her to send to New Bedford. After completing the task of discharging our oil the crew were again given liberty. The captain discharged the second and third mates and shipped others in their places.

From there we sailed for the South Sea Islands, south of the equator. We first sighted the Caroline Islands. We went ashore and traded hard bread, cloth and other things (the captains of whalers usually carry articles to trade with the natives) with the natives, for cocoanuts, pigs, chickens and other eatables. We cruised among the islands for a period of three months, going ashore on several of them, but not getting any whales during the time. We then sailed for the Marquesas group. Seeing two whalers at anchor in Magdalena Bay we ran in and came to an anchor.

We then took on wood and water. The island at this time being inhabited by cannibals (wild Kanakas), we traded old boats to them for wood and let them use the ship's axes to cut it with. While cutting wood for us, one of the natives, not being skilled in the art, cut his leg just above the ankle. In seeing one of their friends badly hurt they all clustered around him. Several began rubbing his leg as hard as they could from the knee down, which caused the man to bleed to death in a very short time. While rubbing his leg his comrades were calling him a great brave in their own tongue.

After he was dead they placed him in a sitting position, placed his old flint-lock gun (traded for with some whale-ship) between his knees with his hands grasping it. A woman then sat down beside him, and began fanning him to keep the flies away.

We stayed there about three weeks, and when we left he was still in the same position, and how much longer he sat there I am unable to say. When we left he was all bloated almost out of recognition.

While we were there the ship Europa and barque Nerva were in for wood and water, and for some reason the natives seized the boat belonging to the Europa and

refused to give it up. The three captains held a consul-
tation on the subject and concluded to fire on the town.
Accordingly our ship, the Marcia, was hauled in shore as
close as was deemed advisable; we then put springs on our
cable fore and aft to hold her in position. We then got
our old cannon from the hold and loaded her, putting in
old nails, spikes, bits of iron, in fact, anything that would
do any damage, and let her go. We fired, I should judge,
about fifty times, when the old chief was seen coming
off to us in his canoe. We ceased firing and he came on
board, and as soon as he stepped on deck we seized and
held him until the boat was delivered up to the owners.
A Kanaka that was on board was dispatched on shore to
tell the natives of the situation, and very soon the boat
was seen making for the Europa. After she was delivered
we let the old chief go, and as soon as he was well away
from the ship we hove up anchor and left, not daring to
stay there any longer, not knowing what the natives might
do. We started for Revolution Bay. This bay is in the
Island of Wacohoo, one of the same group. Here again
we had liberty, the captain giving us cloth, flints and
other things to trade instead of money, as the natives
there had no use for money. While some were on shore
others were painting the ship and making other necessary
repairs.

Albicores and skipjacks are very abundant among these
islands, and we would catch a number of large ones and
salt them down. It is good sport catching them. All you
want is a piece of strong wire bent in the shape of a
hook. Tie a white rag to it and drop it overboard. It
hardly touches the water before they grab it. As they
usually swim along close to the top of the water they are
on the lookout for something to eat. Many of them are
very large, weighing fifty or more pounds. I should

judge their flesh is far superior to our native cod. And again another dish that sharpens the appetite of a sailor is porpoise balls. When the lookout at masthead cries out porpoises, right under you will see an officer or boat steerer grab a harpoon and make it fast to the jib down-haul, or any rope handy, and climb out on the martingale (the span chains under the jib boom) and wait for a good opportunity. As soon as it presents itself he lets go at once, and if fortunate enough to strike him the crew soon have him on deck, when he is easily killed and hung in the rigging, where the cook can get at him. The cook usually cuts off a large quantity of the best part of him, and after chopping it quite fine, seasons it well and rolls it up in balls (like fish balls), and bakes or fries them, and they are very palatable, and I would not mind having some for my breakfast in the morning.

While the ship was at anchor here I and one other of the crew and one from another whaler took leg-bail for the mountains, not caring to stay aboard any longer. The natives soon got after us, setting the tall dry grass on fire to drive us out, thinking we were in among it, but were unsuccessful in dislodging us, as we were not there. We remained in the mountains two days and nights, when we went to another village about ten miles from where our ship was anchored. On arriving at the village we saw only two men, but there were quite a number of women. They acted as though they were pleased to see us, and would jabber to each other, probably wondering where we came from. Presently I noticed the two men talking quite earnestly, and occasionally looking in the direction we had come, and shortly after they went to the shore and started off in a canoe. I was suspicious at once, and made up my mind that they were on the way to inform our captain about us and get a reward. I spoke to my com-

WHALING SHIP MARCIA LEAVING NEW BEDFORD IN 1857

panions about it, but they only laughed at my fears,
saying, "Don't fear; they will never blow on us; we are
all right now." The more I thought of it the more
determined I was that I was right, and as it was nearly
time for the boat to return, if such was the case, I told
my companions I was going up to the water hole, where
we drank on our way down, to get a drink, advising them
to follow me, but they remained firm and I went alone.
After quenching my thirst, as it was very hot then (and
anyone not used to the climate wants to drink all the
time), I went higher up, probably three hundred yards,
and lay down where I could watch the approach of any
boat. In about an hour, I should judge, I saw our ship's
boat come in and take my companions back to the ship,
just as I thought they would. I lay very quiet, and soon
heard the two natives hunting for me with a dog. He
came quite close several times, so near, in fact, that I could
hear him sniff, sniff, trying to smell me out. But not
finding me they soon gave it up. The sun was scorching
hot, and how I stood it I don't know; but as soon as
darkness settled over the island I again went to the water
hole and quenched my thirst. And after the intense heat
of the day it is a wonder I was not sick from drinking so
much. After satisfying my thirst I started up the moun-
tain and down the other side, and as I noticed a sort of
cave I crawled in and slept through the remainder of the
night. I do not know how large it was or whether there
was anything in it, as I did not explore it, but left as soon
as daylight broke. While wandering along I espied
several cocoanut trees, whereupon I decided to climb one
and get some of them. A cocoanut tree is not a very
easy tree to climb, as there are no branches to take hold
of, all the foliage being in a bunch at the top. But I
succeeded in climbing one and gathered several of the

nuts, which, in my hungry state, were very delicious. After
I finished eating them I went a short distance, and again
lay down out of sight in the tall grass. And very soon I
heard two distinct voices, which I concluded were from
two or more of the natives looking for me. (I remained
very quiet and the sound soon ceased.) I remained very
quiet and shady until after dark, when I started towards
the village where we came ashore. The ship was still
at anchor off shore. I made
friends with the king, who hid
me until the vessel sailed; but
as she sailed the next morning
I was not put to much inconvenience. In order to insure
my safety the king had one of
his underchiefs put their sacred
mark on my arm between the
wrist and elbow, which is
called a taboo. Anyone with
this mark on him is safe on
any of these islands. It is a
very queer looking insignia,  and I never could form any
idea what it represented. It is pricked in with sharks or
some other kind of teeth in a very crude manner, and is
not much of a treat to sit and have it done; but if it was to
be the means of my safety I would not object to having
it done, and as I was in their power I could not help
myself anyway, for if they took the notion they would
have tattoed me all over, as most of the natives are
covered with marks hard to distinguish, yet they answer
just as well for them. Their style of dress is generally
unique, being merely a strip of bark soaked in water and
pounded until it is nearly as tough as leather. This is

called a tapper, and is worn around the loins, the rest of their body usually being naked. Some of them trade with vessels and get clothes. Captains usually carry a supply of old clothes on purpose to trade; old-fashioned coats, vests, pants, and old-style hats, including beavers, are a novelty among them. And to see the way some of them put them on would make you split your sides laughing. I have seen the old king make quite a number of changes in one day, and would only wear one article at a time. To see them with pants on and nothing else does not look so queer, but when they put on a vest or coat or an old beaver hat they do look comical enough. Just imagine to yourself how it would seem to you to walk along the street and meet a man all tattooed with India ink, with a strip about the loins and an old high hat on his head, bracing back as though he owned the world, and after passing him meet another naked all but the strip and an old coat, and another with an old vest. I was with them three months, and soon learned to talk quite well, yet I had to laugh whenever I came across them dressed up. Again, many of them shave one side of the face and let the beard grow on the other, which is the most comical part of it all.

Their food consists chiefly of what is called poi, yet pigs and chickens are quite abundant.

Poi is made from breadfruit baked on hot stones and covered with ashes. When done the outside is taken off, when the fruit is pounded up fine and mixed with water, which forms a dough. It is then laid away in a trough or hollow stone to sour, as the more sour it gets the better they like it. They then pound up a cocoanut and squeeze it through the husk, which forms a cream. When the poi is sour enough they sit down and put two fingers in the dough, then in the cream, then into their mouths. I was not used to eating that way, but of course I had to follow suit. The poi as they ate it was too sour for me, so I made a fresh supply for myself as often as I chose.

The natives were at war with each other while I was there, and it would make one laugh to see them get up on the mountains a mile or more apart, and blaze away with their old flint-lock muskets; and they would continue in this manner until one or more is killed or wounded, when peace is again declared. This was in the year 1858.

I had been on the island three months when the barque Greyhound, of Westport, Mass., under command of Captain Cathcart of Nantucket, touched there, and wanted me to go with him. And I was anxious to go, but the old king would not have it; he wanted me to stay with him. I was tired of their mode of life, as I could not write to my parents or friends, and they of course would not know whether I was living or dead; so I meant to join the Greyhound, if possible. At last, after considerable parleying, Captain Cathcart offered the old king some paint, paint oil, hard bread, and lead to make bullets of and a mold to make them in. This touched a tender spot, and the king consented to let me go.

I lost no time in getting ready, as I did not know whether the king would change his mind or not, and I did not feel safe until I was on board; and as soon as I and the captain arrived on board he squared away for the coast of California, and as she had not anchored we only had to sheet home her sails and off we went. We cruised off Cape St. Lucas for a period of about four weeks, but did not see any whales. We went on shore in several places and got clams and mussels and other shellfish. We then sailed for the Maria Island, on the west coast of Mexico. We anchored and went on shore for wood and rabbits. Talk of rabbits, my friends, you

never saw such a sight in your lives unless you have visited this island. They were so thick when I was there
that all we had to do was to knock them right and left
with sticks we carried for that purpose. Some people
will take a gun and one or more dogs and tramp all day
from daylight until dark, or in snow sometimes a foot
deep, and the thermometer many times below zero, just
to get a shot at one or more of these little inoffensive
creatures; and yet here they are as thick as sand fleas in
summer. We stopped the wholesale slaughter after we
had a large pile of them, as we did not want to take the
lives of any more than we wanted to eat. We took on
board, I should judge, between four and five hundred, and
we all had a treat while they lasted. Their tender flesh
was a luxury we had not dreamed of having, but with a
large crew on board they were soon gone, as none, to my
knowledge, ever refused their share when it was sent forward to them. From there we sailed for the Galapagos
Islands. We cruised around a short time without seeing
any whales, when the captain concluded to run to the
island of Albimar. On arriving there we dropped anchor.
After everything was put in shape, about two thirds of
the crew went ashore, taking with us boat sails to make
tents of and water to drink and cook with, as fresh water
cannot be found there. After fitting up our temporary
camp we started for the mountains after turpin, which are
very numerous, and are not found on any other island to
my knowledge. Turpin are a species of turtle, the shell
being in large checks like an alligator skin, and their
flesh is unsurpassed as food for soups and stews; its equal
cannot be found. The liver is far superior to any kind of
meat I ever ate. It is as large as a beef critter's (from a
large one), and is many times superior to it in any way
you choose to cook it. In order to get them we had to

go high up on the mountains, as that seems to be their
roaming ground. They are black in color and move very
slow. We did not disturb the large ones, as we would
have had to kill and cut them up and carry the pieces
down on our backs, as many of them will weigh, I should
think, nearly a half of a ton. So we caught smaller ones,
none weighing over five or six hundred.

We went hunting them every day for a week, and as
they are so clumsy and move so slow, made it an easy
matter to capture them. We built a pen to put them in,
and while on shore lived on them mostly, and used hard
bread from the ship for soups and stews and other ways;
the cook dished it out to us. The small ones we caught
we carried down to camp on our shoulders, but we had
to drag the larger ones. They are perfectly harmless and
never known to bite. We caught about a hundred during
the time. At the close of the week we took them on
board. Their weights would range from about five pounds
to five hundred and over. We put them on deck and
between decks, and let them crawl around as they chose.
It was all of six months before they were all gone. I
never knew one to eat or drink a drop while they were
on board, and yet they looked as fat as a ball of butter
when they were killed. I do not know what they live on
on shore, unless it is grass and bushes or some kind of
herbage that grows on the mountains. They surely do
not drink water, as none is to be found on the island.
The island on the lower portion is mostly pumice stone,
grass being very scarce, unless in some small spot by
itself close to the edge of the mountains. From there
we sailed for the coast of Ecuador, humpback whaling.
We mated with the barque La Grange, Captain Golden,
of Providence, R. I. When vessels mate with each other
it is an understanding between them to unite together in

securing whales, the oil to be divided between them, no matter which ship's boat gets the whale or whales. Many times vessels meet at sea, and on sighting whales one of them will hoist the American flag at the mizzen peak, and if the captain of the other vessel is agreeable to it he will sanction his willingness to mate by hoisting his flag at the mizzen peak also. Then all hands buckle to it and get as many whales as they can.

We anchored about three miles off shore, as humpback whales are caught in shoal water close in shore, and the crews take the boats and cruise for them, a lookout on the ship signaling to them if any are seen from there. The morning is the best time to look for them. It is quite a picnic to get fast to a large bull humpback, as they run very fast, and sometimes you would think there was a large number of cats yowling; then it would change, and one would think a herd of cattle were lowing. These are called singers, and they are well named. Humpback whales are apt many times to capsize a boat, as they are supplied with large fins on each side of their bodies, called topsail yards by sailors. As soon as daylight breaks the crew are on the lookout for them. We got about four hundred barrels all told, which, by mating, only left us about two hundred. And as the season was nearly over we hove up anchor and sailed away for Tombas, on the coast of Peru in South America. We anchored outside and took on a fresh supply of water and sweet potatoes, which are raised in large quantities there, and are generally a grand treat for the sailors; many of them are eaten raw. After putting things in shape we again had liberty, after which we again started for the Callio ground. Just to the south of the Chinchi Islands we cruised, in company with nearly twenty other vessels, for a period of about three months, and only got two small sperm whales during the

time. While cruising there we gammed the barque
Cachelot, A. Houghton and several other whalers, which
was a treat for us, as it is at all times. We exchanged
reading matter and had some good singing and story
telling, and the pipes and tobacco were passed around
quite freely. The two whales caught stowed down about
seventy barrels. After storing our oil below we bade our
friends good-by and good luck and sailed for Valparaiso,
Chili, and on the passage stopped at the Island of Juan
Fernandes, the well-known home of Robinson Crusoe and
his man Friday. We laid off and on three days, and went
ashore after goats, peaches and quinces, or anything we
could get that was good to eat. In the story of Robinson
Crusoe we read that his pets were his goats and kids; but
be that as it may, one to see the great numbers of goats
would not doubt it. We also got a large quantity of claw-
fish close in shore. These fish are similar to our native
lobster, only they have monster claws, from which they
derive their name. Their flesh or meat, as you may call
it, is very nice, and somewhat better, I think, than our
lobster.

We also visited the famous cave, the home of Robinson
Crusoe. This cave extends into the bank forty or fifty
feet, and is about eight or ten feet wide and about ten feet
high in the center. While there gazing into the cave my
mind reverted to the stories I had read and heard related
about this famous place and its occupants, little dreaming
that I should ever see or enter it; yet there I was, and I
felt very much pleased and grateful to our captain for
stopping and allowing us to visit it. We then continued
on to Valparaiso, six hundred miles away. On the way
we sighted whales, and by lowering and working hard
succeeded in capturing one, and while cutting him in the
weather grew heavy and the wind blew very hard, which

caused us to lose the head. The carcass gave us about eighty barrels. On our arrival at Valparaiso the captain ordered the vessel on the dry docks, to repair the copper and make other necessary repairs. I got my discharge there and received my wages, which, if I remember aright, was one dollar and fifty cents; a large sum of money for all my hard work. I remained ashore three or four days and then shipped again, this time on the barque Cachelot, under command of a Captain Perry. So again I found myself afloat bound for the Callio grounds. We took with us two passengers, an Englishman and his wife, a Chilian, whom we were to land on the Island of Juan Fernandes, where they intended to make their home. And as there was only one family of five Spanish people called Chilians living there at the time, I thought to myself they would be quite lonesome there with only five white people there besides themselves. After landing them we proceeded on to the whaling ground. We caught several whales during the season without any serious accident, only a stove boat once in a while; in fact every boat we had was stove more or less during the time. We stowed down about three hundred barrels of sperm oil.

While cruising there the ship Trident of New Bedford, under command of Captain Fisher, of Nantucket, just out from Callio, informed the captain that the owner of the Cachelot, having sent another captain to take command in place of Captain Perry, he was to land at Valparaiso; and the steamer he came on stopped at Callio for coal, and Captain Fisher of the Trident saw and talked with him, and, as was natural, asked him what vessel he was after, and was informed that he was after the Cachelot. After recruiting his vessel he put to sea, and sighting us ran down for a gam, his main object being to inform Captain Perry of the object of the arrival of the new captain. Our cap-

tain was much pleased on account of Captain Fisher noti-
fying him of the transaction about to take place. So
instead of going to Valparaiso he ran into Callio, and sold
about one hundred and fifty barrels of oil while laying off
and on. We put the oil on board of lighters and towed
them nearly in shore, when we cast off the lines and let
them go, so the American consul could not claim the oil.
We then ran a little further in and came to an anchor.
After the sails were furled and rigging coiled up and the
ship put in shape, the captain went on shore and delivered
up his papers to the American consul. That night the
boarding-house runners came on board and coaxed us to
come to their house to board. And the whole crew, myself included, agreed to go, which we did, and in less than
one week we were all shanghaied on board of a large merchant ship bound for Queenstown, Ireland, for orders, and
we soon were notified that we were in debt to the ship
seventy-five dollars. She was the Francis A. Palmer, of
New York, Captain Richardson, and was two thousand
tons burthen. This was in the year 1860. Everything
went well until we were about a week out, when we were
put on a short allowance of food. We had plenty of work
to do and very little to eat. We were loaded with Peru-
vian Guano, not a very sweet-smelling cargo. On account
of the short allowance of food I used to go down between
decks and steal hard bread and stow it away in my berth in
order to get enough to eat. We were about four months
and twenty days on the passage, which was a very rough
one all the way. During the passage three of our topsails
were blown clear from the bolt ropes; this was off the
Western Islands. From Queenstown we were ordered to
London to discharge. After discharging the cargo we
were discharged ourselves, receiving the munificent sum of
about twenty-five dollars for all our hard work.

I stayed in London until my money was gone, then shipped again on the barque Charles Edwin, Captain Littlejohn, of Portland, Me. We went to the north of England to the city of Shields, to load coal for Havana, Cuba.

We had a very rough passage, having to lay the vessel to several times. On our arrival the crew had to hoist out the coal by hand in small baskets and dumped it into lighters alongside. While discharging the coal the vessel was chartered to load sugar at Cardness for New York. After discharging the coal the vessel was thoroughly cleansed to receive the cargo of sugar. While at Cardness the rebel steamer, with the rebel commissioners Mason and Slidell, arrived.

This was at the beginning of the War of 1861. There were several vessels there at the time flying the Southern or rebel flag.

We finished loading and sailed for New York, making the passage in five days; and during the passage we were hove to in a gale in the Gulf Stream about eighteen hours; this was in the month of November of 1861.

It was quite a sight on our arrival to see the outskirts of the city covered with tents, and the city was full of soldiers. I began to think that the North meant business, as everywhere I went I was sure to meet soldiers, the city being fairly alive with them.

I left the vessel there and returned to my home in New Bedford.

CHAPTER II.

AS A MAN-O'-WARSMAN AND SOLDIER.

AFTER having been from home so long I did not feel at all contented with the slow, humdrum life around home, so my stay was short, especially as the war had begun and everything was excitement everywhere; so after remaining at home a few days, the weather being very cold, as it was now December, I enlisted in Uncle Sam's navy and was at once ordered on board the receiving ship Ohio, at the Charlestown Navy Yard, near Boston, and then donned the uniform of the man-o'-warsman. I remained on board of her for a period of two weeks, when I was transferred to the receiving ship Princeton at Philadelphia; about three hundred others were transferred at the same time.

We went from Charlestown to Philadelphia on the steamship Kensington, and were four days on the passage; the weather was very cold and it snowed most of the time, but we had a very jolly crowd on board and plenty of singing and story-telling, so we did not heed the weather.

January the 18th I was again transferred to the flagship Hartford, she being the flagship of Admiral (at that time Commodore) Farragut, one of our most brave and noted commanders in the Union army or navy; on the 20th of the same month we steamed down to the powder station and took on powder and shell.

As soon as we finished loading we started for Hampton Roads, at the entrance of the Chesapeake Bay in Virginia; from there we went to Hilton Head, in South Carolina, Havana, Cuba, Key West, Florida, Ship Island; and from there to the mouth of the Mississippi River. After the arrival of the fleet of vessels under Commodore Farragut we started up the Mississippi, the Hartford taking the lead; our intentions were to make an attack on forts Jackson and St. Phillips.

On arriving within a suitable distance, we began firing, and kept up the attack for six days and nights without cessation, the whole fleet throwing about twenty-eight hundred shells every twenty-four hours, or a total of sixteen thousand and eight hundred during the time. Such a sight and noise I never saw nor heard before, and I hope I never shall see nor hear again. Shells were bursting everywhere, and the nights were nearly as light as day with the quick succession of flashes from the cannons' mouths, and the thick smoke rolled away in clouds. It was a magnificent display of fire, but the danger coupled with it left no chance for anyone to stop to admire it, as death and destruction were in the air, and none of us knew when a stray shot or shell would take us from this vale of tears and launch us into eternity. We on the Hartford were in such a position as to be unable to use any of our guns except our large Dahlgreen, or bow gun, as it was called, as none of the others could be used with any effect, yet our broadside guns were loaded and manned ready to fire as an opportunity offered.

About two o'clock in the morning of the 24th of April we were ordered to get under weigh to pass the forts. We were all ordered to lie down flat on deck out of sight of the enemy, and at the command to rise and fire, and to load and fire as often as possible until told to stop ; at the command to fire it was meant for our whole broadside to blaze away.

When the broadsides of the fleet rang out on the air it was enough to fairly burst the drums in a person's ears ; the flash, flash from the muzzles of the guns were almost enough to blind or dazzle one's eyes ; and the continuous bursting of shells, and the whistle and swish, swish of the chain shot, fired to cut our rigging and hulls to pieces, gave none of us a chance to stop to think or collect our thoughts; everything was bustle and commotion, and everybody acted as though they thought everything at that time depended on them. The sight was indeed appalling, and any of the persons that took part in it will surely remember it to their dying day. Ofttimes as my mind reverts to it I seem to almost see and hear it over again.

During the attack the rebels were launching large fire-rafts from different points and would start them so they would be pretty sure to run into the fleet attacking the forts, several of the fleet got on fire from them, but the flames were soon extinguished. One of them was drifting direct towards us, and we tried hard to clear it; our helm was put hard aport to try and run clear from it, and by doing so we struck on a shoal and immediately came to a standstill, which put us in a bad way, as the raft lay on our port side and threatened to destroy us by setting our vessel on fire. We fired a whole broadside at it to try and sink it if possible, but could not do so. Our rigging was on fire at this time, as the fire-raft lay close to us and hugged the side of our vessel with a determination to stay until we were destroyed, but we were not so easily destroyed; we fought the flames with a desperate will to outdo the rebels, but it was hot work, yet we held to it to the last, and at last succeeded.

The Commodore paced the poop deck as unconcerned as though nothing had happened, but would occasionally cast a glance up at the flames which had started up our rigging. He seemed as cool and collected as though he was taking a stroll on a beautiful May morning, and showed himself to be the brave commander he really was.

We at last succeeded in backing the vessel off, and the fire-raft was set adrift. Our loss during the attack on the forts was three killed and ten wounded, with thirty-two shots in our hull and rigging. We continued on to quarantine to bury our dead; we then steamed up the river towards New Orleans; when about eight miles below the Chalmette batteries opened fire upon us, and we could only return the fire with our bow gun. We lost one man. The river was full of fire-rafts, but we ran clear of them all, and ran in and anchored off abreast of New Orleans, where we remained until the arrival of General Butler's command.

The city was in an uproar on our arrival, and the wharves were thronged with people. Two officers were dispatched on shore to demand of the mayor the surrender of the city. They went on their perilous expedition without an escort, and as they arrived in their boat alongside of the pier they found that they would have to fairly squeeze their way through the crowd collected there. Nothing daunted, however, they clambered upon the wharf, and on glancing right and left saw that all the slum and dissipated men and women, as well as the well to do, were gathered there, plainly showing by their looks and actions their hatred for the Yankees. As soon as the crowd saw them step on shore they hooted and hissed like maniacs, and such a discord of voices as was heard was enough to make a brave man quail.

As the officers stepped on the shore they demanded of the crowd to know where the mayor lived or could be found. At this the crowd broke out afresh, saying "down with the Yankees," "shoot them," "hang them to a lamp post," and so on, but no one offered the required information, and they proceeded in elbowing their way through the infuriated mob of human beings.

We could see them from the vessel, and saw that they were not molested, but soon they disappeared from view.

None of us could tell what their fate might be, but our guns were loaded with grape and canister and manned ready to open fire upon the mob at the first sign of any attempt to disturb them. These two brave officers were Captain Bailey and Lieutenant Perkins. It was a daring deed, and we should all be proud to have such brave and loyal heroes on our banner. Why they were not attacked by the frenzied mob I am unable to say, unless it was the brave, determined manner they stepped ashore with. After a short stay on shore they were again seen heading towards their boat, and as before had to fairly elbow their way through the mob, but as before they were not assaulted. After getting into their boat they soon reached the vessel, and as they stepped on board they were met by a crew of brave men that knew how to applaud a brave act, and their welcome back was a rousing cheer from the whole fleet.

Shortly after their arrival on board Captain Charles H. Bell, with a guard of marines, was ordered on shore with two boat howitzers. On arriving at the pier they were met with the same kind of reception as the other officers, but he, with his guards, made direct for the State House. On arriving there the marines were drawn up into line, with their weapons pointed at the crowd, with orders to fire at the first sign of interference. Captain Bell then ascended to the roof of the building and tore down the rebel flag and hoisted in its place the stars and stripes.

The crowd stood spellbound, as though frozen to the spot, and not a voice was heard for several minutes; such daring had completely taken their breath away. That was bearding the lion in his den in earnest.

And, strange to say, not a shot was fired, which proved beyond a doubt that such daring had completely unmanned them. The captain and his escort then marched to the Custom House, where the same performance was enacted, the crowd eagerly watching every move, but not lifting so much as a finger to stop it. Every man and boy on board the fleet cheered lustily the brave acts of our comrades. It was almost like baring the breast to a duelist and inviting him to take your life. None of us expected they would return alive, but with the courage of a lion they dared to do or die, and do it they did, and they should not be forgotten.

After hoisting the stars and stripes on the Custom House Captain Bell descended to the ground, and with a defiant, never-to-be-forgotten look ordered the marines to march towards their boat, and they were soon on board, the heroes of the hour. Tears could be seen on many faces, tears of joy to welcome as comrades such daring heroes.

Shortly after the fleet started up the river toward Vicksburg. When about eight miles above New Orleans went ashore on the left bank and spiked twenty-nine guns. We were informed that our fleet had sunk seven rebel gunboats in the attack on Forts Jackson and St. Phillips.

We continued on as far as Baton Rouge, where we took on coal. While coaling up some of our officers were fired upon by guerrillas, wounding one of them. We then fired four or five shots into the town. After coaling up we proceeded to Vicksburg, and arrived there June 25th, 1862, and began bombarding the town. Their fortifications were spread all along the hills, about fifty yards apart, and about one and one-half miles in from shore and about two hundred and fifty feet up from the level, which made it a very strong fortification, and was called the Gibraltar of the West, and to have seen it you would have said it was rightly named.

We passed up very slowly, our steam being down to about eight pounds. We stopped several times on that account. We continued to fire until ordered to stop; one of our crew was killed and eighteen wounded. We continued on and anchored among Admiral Davis's fleet.

While anchored there with our fires down the rebel ram Arkansas ran the gauntlet by our fleet, giving us several shots as a parting tribute of her prowess. By not having steam up we could not pursue her, but we gave her a broadside as she passed, several shots taking effect. We got ready that night to pass the forts, and swung our anchors at the yardarm to drop on and grapple the ram Arkansas should we be fortunate enough to get near her, but she did not make her appearance.

While abreast of Vicksburg we were fired upon and a heavy battle was indulged in. Shot and shell were whistling everywhere, and the flashes of the large guns made the night as light as day. The firing was continuous. George H. Loundsberry, master's mate, had his head taken clear from his body, as though cut off with a razor; his body fell to the deck, but his head was never found. Two others were killed and six wounded during the engagement.

After passing the Gibraltar, Vicksburg, we continued down the river. Arriving off Grand Gulf we were fired upon by guerrillas, and after we passed the town was burned by the fleet. The town of Donaldsonville was also burned.

We continued on to New Orleans, where I left the Hartford and took my effects on shore.

On arriving on shore I enlisted in the First Louisiana Infantry, under General Butler, many of the regiment being those formerly of the garrison in Forts Jackson and St. Phillips, in the rebel service. We were mustered into service August 25th, 1862, and went into camp at Camp Carney, to drill and prepare ourselves for battle.

From there we were ordered to Donaldsonville, about eighty miles above. We remained there during the winter of 1862. We built a fort there and mounted eight guns; we also dug a trench around it. We named the fort Fort Butler. While we were there General Banks was sent to relieve General Butler. General Banks took command of the Nineteenth Army Corps.

In the spring of 1863 we formed an expedition to go up the Red River. We marched from Donaldsonville to Brazier City, where we boarded transports and went across the lake and landed at a place called Irish Bend, in Louisiana, where we had a battle, our major being the first one wounded. The fight lasted four or five hours, and bullets flew thick and fast during the time.

I do not remember how many were killed and wounded, but the number was large. In the afternoon the rebels retreated; we followed along the river where they had a gunboat named the Cotton, and for fear she would fall into our hands they set her on fire and blew her up.

We kept on towards Alexandria, driving the rebels ahead of us all the way. We marched through the day and went into camp at night, when pickets would be posted, and our guns stacked handy to reach in case of necessity, then we would be off for fence rails to sleep on and make fires with. After supper was over we would start out foraging for something good for breakfast. One place we came across we saw about twenty cattle in a barn-yard, and before daylight every one of them was killed and dressed ready to cook for breakfast. The owner of them was so dumbfounded, when he arose in the morning, he could hardly speak, but cried like a child. It was hard to see a strong man crying, but we had about eighteen thousand hungry men to feed, and it took considerable to do it. We would take anything we came across, pigs, chickens, ducks, goats, or anything eatable, potatoes, cabbages, turnips, corn, or anything we wanted.

The next morning we again set out, and after marching all day we camped about sundown. Several of us went to a planter's house, and seeing a flock of geese in the yard I asked the owner for one, which he indignantly refused; whereupon I shot one of them and picked him up and started off with him. He stood and looked hard at me, but didn't open his mouth. I don't know how many geese he had left in the morning, but I don't believe he had any, for as soon as the boys saw them they would want and would have them. The last of that night finished up our foraging on that trip, as we reached Alexandria.

We remained there about four days and started towards Shreveport. We had tramped about twelve miles west of Alexandria, when we picked up a quantity of cotton which we seized. We then returned over the same route until within a few miles of the Mississippi River, when we took transports and went down the Red River about twelve miles; when we reached the Mississippi, went down a short distance and landed. When within about twelve miles of Port Hudson, we dug trenches for a distance of about eight miles and laid siege to the city.

My readers may think it strange that we should march in such a roundabout way, but our object was to draw the troops and forces away from Port Hudson, so we would have an easier victory over them and take the place from them. We practiced all the tricks we (our commander) could think of to draw their attention from our object, as skillful manœuvering was better than bloodshed. On the 27th of June, 1863, we made a charge upon Port Hudson, and we found them better fortified than we anticipated. They had cut down all the trees around their stronghold, which made it hard work for us, as we had to climb over the fallen trees, as they had been left just as they fell, and as fast as we undertook to charge upon them we were repulsed, losing heavily. As fast as any of our boys showed themselves their sharpshooters would pick them off, and we soon found that in order to keep from being utterly wiped out was to drop behind the fallen trees and lie there out of sight, which we did, as it was no use to throw our lives away, for nothing could be gained by so doing.

It must have been a queer sight to them to see us crawling and scrambling over trees and branches and stumps, trying to get near to them. We lay where we dropped until after dark, when we crawled back to our trenches. Our colonel was killed in the engagement and our total loss was three or four thousand. I was fortunate in not receiving a scratch, yet the boys were falling all around me, as the bullets flew like hailstones. It is not a pleasant thing to see your comrades dropping all around you, many of them dead before striking the ground, and none of us knew but our turn would come next. Yet we undauntedly kept up the siege, with more or less shots exchanged, until the 8th of July, when they surrendered to us. This surrender was to General Banks, the commander of our Corps.

While we held siege over Port Hudson the rebels from Texas made an attack upon Fort Butler at Donaldsonville. Upon being informed about it we boarded transports and went there and landed and marched on to bayou La Flusch, four miles below, and went into camp; and the following afternoon the rebs made an attack upon us at a place called Coxes Plantation. The rebels meant business and intended to rout us; several of our command were killed and wounded; as they pressed us so hard we retreated toward Donaldsonville. The rebs, thinking we were drawing them into a trap, and not caring to be hemmed in, they left for Texas again. They did not know that Port Hudson had surrendered, and, as Vicksburg was sieged at the time Port Hudson was taken, was the means of cutting off all chances for supplies; so, on account of this, they surrendered to us, but they were stubborn and held out as long as they could.

After the surrender of Vicksburg we went into camp, and while we were camped there we made several runs up the Mississippi River on transports, the army going into quarters in several places in Louisiana.

We remained near Donaldsonville until the spring of 1864, acting as garrison for Fort Butler.

The second Red River campaign was started under General Banks, and we were relieved by a colored company, so we left for Brazier City to join our troops. We took transports to cross the river, and then took up the line of march towards Alexandria. We marched about twelve miles a day and went into camp at night, and each night on the line of march the planters were minus pigs, chickens, ducks and other eatables.

The fleet of gunboats were following up the river while we were marching on land. We at last arrived in Alexandria all right, and after a short stay we started again towards Shreveport. About twelve miles from Grandico, at a place called Pleasant Hill, we had a heavy battle and got badly whipped. We lost all of our artillery and ammunition train with provisions, besides small arms. A great many were killed and wounded and taken prisoners. Towards night the firing ceased and we went into camp.

In the night we were reinforced with about fifteen thousand men, under command of Major A. J. Smith of the Thirteenth Army Corps.

The next morning the rebs made another attack on us. They little dreamed what a reception they would receive from us, through being reinforced during the night. But they were not long kept in suspense as we whipped them far worse than they did us. We mowed them down like grass upon the farmer's scythe, and they lost no time in retreating, and we were fortunate in recovering everything taken from us during our first engagement with them. After completely routing them we went back to Grandico. While there we built a fortification of logs for protection.

The water was falling so fast in the river the gunboats were in danger of running aground, so they retreated down the river toward Alexandria, the rebs firing at them all the way. We again took up the line of march. The first day we marched forty-two miles without a rest. Upon arriving at Alexandria the water was falling so rapidly the gunboats could not get over the falls, on account of which it was decided to build a dam in order to keep enough water above to allow them to get over the falls. We built the dam, which was a success, but coupled with plenty of hard work. We built the dam in eight days. The falls are about a mile in length and interspersed with jagged rocks, which looked very uninviting for a vessel to try to run through. We ran out and sank four large coal barges at the end of the falls, from the right bank of the river. Cribs filled with stone were then run out to meet the barges, all of which was fully accomplished, notwithstanding there was a current running at the rate of nine miles an hour, threatening to sweep everything before it.

At the end of the eighth day the water had risen so many of the vessels could come down; in another day it would be high enough to allow all to come down, but, unfortunately, on the next day the pressure of the water was so great as to sweep away two of the barges of stones. It was a sight to see (and we were where we had a good view of it all) those large gunboats go over those falls.

As each one approached to run the gauntlet you could almost hear a pin drop, but as they passed safely over the falls cheer upon cheer would ring from a thousand throats at once. There were at that time on the fleet and on the shore about thirty thousand Yankee soldiers and sailors, each and every one much interested in the safety of the gunboats, as a great deal depended on them at all times.

After the fleet had passed the falls we all followed down the Red River. The city of Alexandria was set or got on fire in some way, and the flames could be seen very plain for a distance of four or five miles.

We marched on down to Atchafalaya, and in order to cross the river the transports were drawn up in line alongside of each other, forming a regular pontoon bridge, as we all marched over them and arrived safely on the other side. We marched from there to Moganzie Landing, on the Mississippi River.

We built a fort there and named it Fort Moganzie. We all camped there about a month. While there Major-General Canby was sent out to take command from Major-General Banks. We were ordered from there to New Orleans, and on arriving there we went into camp. Then the Nineteenth Army Corps were ordered to go up the Potomac, and we were sent to Fort Butler, at Donaldsonville, and stayed there until the close of the war, and at the close we were ordered down to New Orleans to be mustered out of service.

On the 16th of July, 1865, while at Donaldsonville, I was on provost guard, and was dispatched to go to New Orleans with rebel prisoners. We went on transports, and, as it was night when we arrived, and very dark, the plank that was run out to walk ashore on was not wide enough for me to see, so overboard I went. My gun sank, and away went my cap, and the only way I got out was by following the sound of the voices on shore; but I managed to get on shore, and delivered up the prisoners to the provost marshal and returned to the fort.

After I was mustered out of service I stayed in New Orleans about a week, and was presented a free pass to New York.

While the steamer I was in, bound for New York, was off Key West, the boilers gave out. The fires were drawn and the steam blown off; when repairs were made we again started for New York. Off abreast of Charleston they gave out again, when sail was set and we again began repairs. While sailing along in the Gulf Stream we sighted a steamer, when we put up a flag of distress. She proved to be the George Washington, the one I was on being the barque-rigged steamer Blackstone. The George Washington was bound from New Orleans to New York. Our captain asked the other captain to tow us in, but as they were a mail steamer they could not do so; but he consented to take all the passengers in, so I went on board and soon arrived in New York. From there I went to my home in New Bedford.

CHAPTER III.

TO DIFFERENT PARTS OF THE COUNTRY.

My stay at home, as on the previous occasion, was very short, as I again shipped on a small vessel carrying freight from one port to another. We contracted for the season to carry oil and grain between New Bedford and Albany, New York. I remained aboard of her until late in the fall, and joined another one bound from New Bedford to Georgetown, D. C., and loaded with coal there for Sandwich, and again returned to New Bedford, where I remained through the winter.

In the spring of 1866, I again shipped on the brig Morning Star, of Providence, R. I., bound for Montevideo, South America. It was in the month of March that we sailed, and the weather was very raw and cold. The first five days we experienced very heavy weather, and had to throw overboard our deck load of lumber, as the vessel was leaking very badly. The heavy seas striking her, and she being loaded so heavily, was the means of straining her and set her to leaking, and all the men that could be spared were pumping continually to try and keep her free. When the wind moderated and the seas went down we managed to free her from water when everything went along quite smoothly, until heavy weather again set in, and again she began leaking, the crew pumping all the time. About twenty days out we were struck by a heavy gale, which played sad havoc with us, as we lost our foretopmast and foreyard, topgallant and royal yard.

We then rigged up a jury mast and ran into Rio Janeiro, where we had a general overhauling. After everything was put in shape we again started on our trip south, and had very heavy weather all the time until we arrived at

Montevideo, which caused us to lay the vessel to, and man the pumps, in order to stay afloat. It was during a heavy gale that we ran in as far as possible, which brought us deep into the mud.

We remained there about a month when we were ordered up the river, about three hundred miles to Buenos Ayres. The passage was made in three days, when we anchored about seven miles from the city, as at that time large vessels generally anchored from fifteen to twenty miles below the city.

We remained there about five months. During the time we experienced two severe pamperos. The first one drove seventeen vessels ashore, making total wrecks of all of them, as they went to pieces in a short time, and the second drove nine more ashore, totally wrecking them all. Many anchors were lost there; not any of the vessels that were wrecked had probably less than two down, to try to hold the vessel. But they proved of little avail, as they all drove ashore, which left the anchors on the bottom. A new side-wheel passenger steamer named the Oriento, a very large boat, started on her trip from Buenos Ayres to Montevideo, and as the water was shoal she was so unfortunate as to strike one or more of the anchors on the bottom, which stove a large hole in her bottom. She soon filled and sank, and on account of the water being shoal her deck remained two or three feet out of the water. She sank about two and one-half miles from shore. As soon as we saw what had happened, we lowered our boat and put in a diving suit and apparatus and started for her, the captain luckily having them aboard at the time.

Our cargo consisted of material for constructing a marine railway, and as diving suits are used in placing them we carried them also; and it was fortunate for the crew of the steamer that we were there at the time. As soon as we boarded the steamer, our captain made arrangements with the steamer's captain to stop up the hole in her bottom. I was asked if I would don the suit and go down on the bottom and investigate the real damage. Being young and venturesome, I quickly volunteered to do so.

I put on the suit, which was heavily weighted with lead and was so heavy I could hardly walk, and when they were ready to put on the large helmet one of our crew began pumping air to me to enable me to breathe. It was a queer sensation to have to depend on a machine to furnish air to breathe, as that was the only means I had to get any after the helmet was adjusted. When I went down to the bottom I found it no trouble at all to move about as I chose; and upon investigation I found that the bottom of the steamer was so flat and the bottom so hard, I could not discover the hole made by the sunken anchor.

I remained down several hours, without any success whatever. I then gave the signal to be drawn up, and after removing the helmet I called for a shovel and hoe and again descended, and began digging in order to locate the place that was stoven. I was digging most of the time for several days, and as the bottom was so hard it was slow work. I had not succeeded in locating the spot when another pampero visited us and swept the steamer's upper works entirely away, which made a complete wreck of her, on account of which we abandoned the undertaking. The steamer was then thrown on the hands of the under-writers, who sold her as she lay at auction.

About a month after this we were ordered across the river about thirty miles to a place called Colonia, to put down the marine railway. This place is in the Oriental Republic.

We discharged our cargo on shore, and were then or-dered on shore to help construct it, as we carried the carpenters with us that were to build it. While we were building the railway, the captain shipped some Spaniards (and sailed the vessel to Montevideo, where he sold her at auction). As soon as I heard of it I refused to work on shore as I wanted to go on the vessel. The captain refused to let me go on board, and put me in the caliboose (jail). After he had sold her he came to me to see if I would go to work. Upon my refusing to do so he let me out, as he had to pay my board while I was there.

After I got out I stayed around four or five days and then started on foot for Montevideo, three hundred miles away. In some places there was quite a good road, and in others there was none. I did not know where I would come out, as it was all guess-work and nothing to guide me, but I kept on going; some days I walked twenty or more miles without seeing a house of any kind, and when night came on I would place a stone pointing in the direction I was walking, so I would not get turned round after sleeping. It was a very tedious journey all alone. I saw a great many animals on the way, such as gazelles, antelopes, tigers, and hundreds of ostriches. What few people I saw were very good to me, and gave me plenty to eat. I was nine days making the journey, and a lonesome nine days it was, too, and in a strange country. I tried to make the people I met understand that I was bound for Montevideo, and they would point for me, and by going as they pointed I arrived at last, but very footsore and weary, and I was thankful I was there.

As soon as I arrived I called on the American Consul and received the money due me from the vessel, which amounted to about one hundred and fifty dollars. I remained there about two weeks and then shipped on a whitewash barque bound for New York with a load of hides. These vessels were called whitewash on account of wanting to keep clear from the privateers, by flying the English flag instead of the American flag. The one I shipped on was an American with English colors and hailed from Capetown, but in reality belonged in New York. We were sixty-three days on the passage, which was a very rough one, head winds and gales most of the time. We arrived in New York in March, 1867.

I remained in New York several days and returned to New Bedford. I then, after a short stay at home, shipped on a coasting schooner for the balance of the summer. In the fall I went to the West Indies, returning in the spring of 1868. I then joined a wrecking party and made a business of diving in a diving suit. I patched a great many vessels ready for raising, cut and cleared the rigging from others, hooked on anchors, chains and a hundred and one other things that I chanced to find on the bottom. I continued in this capacity until about July, 1869, when I again went to New York and shipped as second mate of the barque Fannie, bound for Havre, France, with a cargo of petroleum oil in barrels. We had a very rough passage and lost several sails.

On arriving we discharged our cargo and took on ballast and sailed for Cardiff, Wales, to load coal for Havana, Cuba. We again had a very rough passage. On arriving, the crew had to discharge the coal in small baskets, by hoisting it out with a winch. After discharging we loaded sugar in hogsheads for New York. We arrived there in March, 1870. I left the vessel there and shipped on the schooner Annie A. Whitin. After putting my things on board we started on our passage for English Guinea, Central America; we carried a cargo of breadstuff in the hold and live sheep on deck. Nothing of any importance occurred during the passage. We arrived and discharged our cargo and took on a return cargo of sugar for New York. We made the trip in about fifty days.

On our arrival in New York, I left and took my things on shore and again shipped, this time on the brig Gazelle, of Harrington, Maine, commanded by a Captain Cole. I shipped with him as his mate. We then began loading coal for Boston. We made the run without accident of any kind. We sailed from Boston, after unloading the cargo of coal, in ballast for Bangor, Maine. On our arrival we began taking in our cargo of orange box shooks for Palermo, in the Island of Sicily. We finished loading and started for our destination, nearly four thousand miles away.

On our way we stopped at Gibraltar several days and then started again for our destination. The passage at times was quite unpleasant, but nothing of any serious nature occurring. On our arrival we discharged our cargo in lighters, as there was no place to land except in small boats. We took a return cargo of oranges, lemons and sulphur for Boston, Mass. From there we went to Porto Rico, in the West Indies, and discharged our cargo of breadstuffs in three different ports on the island. We then took in ballast and sailed for Turk's Island after a cargo of salt; loaded and proceeded to New York; arrived and discharged the cargo, and took on a general cargo for Galveston, Texas. We took on a cargo of cotton for a return to New York. After discharging the cargo of cotton we took on a cargo of naphtha for Stockholm, Sweden, up the Baltic Sea, by the route of the north of Scotland.

We had a nice passage and arrived safe and sound, discharged our cargo, and began loading iron for New York, which took us nearly a month. After completing loading we set sail for New York. We sailed down the Baltic Sea, across the North Sea, and out through the English Channel. After passing Scilly Islands, off and in sight of Land's End, England, we encountered heavy westerly gales and heavy weather all the way until within about five hundred miles

of the Grand Banks, off Newfoundland, when we were
struck by a terrible hurricane. The vessel being loaded so
deep, and with a dead weight cargo, made her behave very
bad, the water on deck at times being even with the vessel's
rails. We lay the vessel to under a double-reefed mainsail,
and my readers can form a little idea what the ocean in its
fury is, when I tell you that with our mainsail double-reefed
we were boarded by a heavy sea which struck the mainsail
and tore it into ribbons. After this accident occurred she
labored very hard. If we had a cargo of lumber, or some
other light material, we would have thought nothing about
it, as she would have rode the seas like a duck; but being
loaded with iron was not very pleasant just at this time.

As she lay to she rolled in the trough of the sea,—as
though she would never rise from it. We were expecting
all the time she would founder, and for fear she would we
tried our best to keep her afloat. We got the cargo gaff
and hook, a small anchor, and lashed it to the gaff, and
made a hawser fast to the bridle on the gaff, and dropped it
over the weather quarter, making the hawser fast to a bit
forward; and as the vessel drifted to the leeward the gaff
pulled out ahead. This did not seem to do much good, so
we took tarpaulins and put them in the main rigging, and
then unbent the main staysail and set it for a storm trysail
on the mainmast; and as this didn't seem to do any good,
we began to throw some of the cargo of iron overboard.

We threw overboard about twelve tons the first day, yet
she continued to roll and slat about, so that our fore topgallant mast, with yards and sails, went by the board.
This hurricane held on for seventy-two hours, when the
weather began to moderate. As soon as we deemed it advisable to remove our main hatches we did so, and threw
overboard about forty tons more of our cargo. As we had
met with such an accident to our masts and rigging, the

captain concluded to run in to Fayal, to repair damages; and as we had a strong fair wind we made the run in four days, when we anchored in the harbor of Norta Fayal. We put down three anchors to make sure and hold her, as we had met with enough misfortune already. We had a survey on the vessel, and were recommended to discharge our cargo in order to make the necessary repairs, and put her in shape to continue the passage.

The cargo was sent on shore in lighters, on account of which we were ten days or more before it was all out. After completing repairs we took on our cargo again and sailed for New York. Before leaving, the American Consul put seven sailors that were ashore there on his hands from a condemned vessel, on board with us to bring to the United States. We had a very rough passage, but luckily without accident. The run was made in forty-two days. On arriving we discharged the cargo, and after everything was put on shore and the vessel put in shape, I left and took my effects on shore.

I remained in New York several days, when I shipped again, this time on the brig Myronus, of Ellsworth, Me., under command of Captain Higgins. This was in July, 1872. We loaded crude petroleum for Marseilles, France. We had a pleasant passage, and made the run in about forty days. We discharged our cargo and loaded tiles for San Fugas, south side of Cuba. These tiles are made of clay, and look like a piece of pipe cut in two in the center. They are used for shingling houses, and are sure to run all the water off that strikes on them, as they form a regular spout. We finished loading on November 21st, 1872. The date is fresh in my memory, as on the following day (it was a gala day for me) I was married on board the vessel at three o'clock in the afternoon. The American Consul, named Price, and the vice consul, came aboard

MRS. CAPT. THOMAS CRAPO.

and performed the ceremony. The bride was a Miss Joanna Styff, of Glasgow, Scotland; and in order to tell you what countrywoman she is I will give you the facts, and, kind reader, you can try to explain the puzzle yourself. She was born in Glasgow, Scotland, Sept. 26, 1854. Her father was a native of Stockholm, Sweden; her mother was an English woman, a native of Newcastle-on-Tyne. When eight years of age her parents moved to Marseilles, France, where she also attended school and is a splendid French scholar. She remained there until the Yankee sailor, Captain Crapo, made her his bride, when we started on our return trip.

We sailed on the 23d, with a nice fair wind for the first three days, down the Mediterranean Sea. My wife was very sea-sick, and home-sick as well, for a week or more, which made it very unpleasant for her; but as she began to get better, she soon seemed like herself again. We then had strong westerly winds, and it took us about twenty days to get down to Gibraltar, and as we could not get through the straits we anchored and waited for a fair wind.

We made ourselves as comfortable as possible, not knowing how long we should have to wait. On the fourth day the wind veered around, when we hove up our anchor and made sail and proceeded on our way, the rest of the passage being very pleasant.

At last we arrived in January, 1873. After discharging the cargo we loaded sugar for New York, my wife remaining on board with me. We arrived in New York and discharged the cargo. After everything was put to rights I took my discharge and, accompanied by my wife, started for my home in New Bedford, where I remained until late in the fall of the same year, when I again shipped as mate on the schooner Annie Tibbets, Captain Curtis, of Harrington, Maine. My wife again accompanied me, as she was a plucky sailor, and wanted to go where I did. We went to Tiverton, Rhode Island, to load fish guano for Philadelphia, Penn. The Captain's wife also accompanied him on this trip. The only drawback to this trip was that Mrs. Crapo did not like the perfume of the cargo, as fish guano is not suitable to anyone's taste, and the smell clings-to your clothing for weeks afterwards. After being on board with it a short time one gets used to it and almost forgets it remains in the clothing, but if I got into a horse-car or passed anyone on the street they could smell it very readily, and would let you know it by turning up their noses.

After discharging this rancid, foul-smelling cargo we loaded coal for New Bedford, Mass., my birthplace. We were taking on the coal at Port Richmond when, in the evening, Mrs. Curtis, the Captain's wife, and my wife and myself started to go uptown, shopping. The place is completely covered with railroad tracks, and trains are coming and going all the time. I proceeded ahead to act as pilot across the tracks, when soon I heard my wife screaming. It seems she was walking behind Mrs. Curtis when her shoe heel caught in a frog in the track, and her screaming probably saved her life, as a train was nearing her on that same track and stopped just before reaching her.

As she screamed, I turned and saw this train coming, when I hurriedly extricated her from her perilous position without accident, but she was badly frightened, and will probably never forget it, as she often speaks of it. After loading the vessel we proceeded on our journey, and as we had good weather, we arrived and discharged our cargo without any accident whatever. After discharging the cargo we hauled alongside the dock, and remained there about two months, as the ice was making fast, as it was very cold.

In the spring of the following year we again sailed, this time for Orient, Long Island, to load fertilizer for Port Royal, South Carolina. We had a good passage as far as the lightship off Port Royal, named the Martin Industry. We arrived off there about ten o'clock in the forenoon and set our colors at our foremast for a pilot. We sailed around all day but none came off to us. At night we shortened sail and let her drift around; but during the night a heavy gale sprung up and the weather was very thick and foggy, on account of which we were blown off shore into the Gulf Stream.

The gale lasted for three days and nights, and it was eight days before we got back to the lightship. We then got a pilot and ran in and discharged. We then loaded railroad ties for New York; arrived and discharged them all right. We then took in ballast for Fernandina, Florida. My wife left the vessel here, and went to her brother's, in New Brunswick, N. J. We had a good passage all the way, and on arriving we discharged the ballast and took on a cargo of ship timber for Harrington, Maine. We had a very rough passage; many times the seas would wash clear across the vessel. We ran in within seven miles of our destination, when owing to the crookedness of the river, we rafted the timbers on shore.

After discharging I left the vessel and went on to New York, where I shipped on a three-masted schooner named the James M. Riley, of Harrington, Maine, under command of a Captain Eaton. I shipped with him as first mate, and we were to load petroleum oil for Cranston, Finland, in Russia. Our course was across the Atlantic to the north of Scotland, across the North Sea, then through the Straits of Elsinor into the Baltic Sea. Our cargo was for St. Petersburg, but as the water was not deep enough to allow us to go there we had to discharge at Cranston,

about fifteen miles below, yet we could see St. Petersburg
quite plain. After discharging we took in ballast of about
thirty tons and sailed towards Cape Britain, New Brunswick.

While sailing down the Baltic Sea we had very heavy
weather and soon found out we did not have in ballast
enough, so we put in to Copenhagen, Denmark, and put
aboard fifty more tons. After it was aboard and properly
trimmed we again started on our passage. We went back
north of Scotland again on our way to Cape Britain. We
experienced very heavy weather all the way, which took
us forty days, when we ran in to New Caledonia, Cape
Britain, where we unloaded our ballast and loaded coal
for New York. The passage was a very rough one and
took us eighteen days. After discharging our cargo we
had the vessel hauled alongside the wharf, where she remained for two months, waiting for a cargo. At last we
chartered to load sugar-box shooks for Cardness, north
side of Cuba; had very heavy weather, and lost our fore-
topmast and jibboom in a gale. While we were discharging, Captain Boynton, a part owner of the vessel, took
command in place of Captain Eaton, and as his wife came
on with him I had mine join us, as it would be pleasant
for the Captain's wife to have company on board, as well
as company for me.

While we were discharging, the two ladies were ashore
most of the time, enjoying themselves and seeing the sights.
After discharging we loaded sugar for New York; had
very heavy weather and snowstorms north of Cape Hatteras. On arriving at Sandy Hook we anchored, and the
heavy ice coming down on us drove us about five miles to
sea. The next morning a towboat came down and offered
to tow us in for one thousand dollars. This was an enor-
mous sum, and made us whistle. At last, after some

parleying, the Captain offered them two hundred dollars, and after due consideration they agreed to take it, so they took our lines and started with us. The tide and ice was against us, and it took them all day to tow us thirty miles. We looked like a floating iceberg instead of a vessel on our arrival at the wharf; everything was ice everywhere. We began to discharge our cargo, which was not a very pleasant job, as the weather was so cold and ice was everywhere.

After discharging the cargo I left the vessel and shipped as first mate on the brig Kaluna, Captain Nash, of Harrington, Maine; my wife also went with me. We loaded a general cargo for Fernandina, Florida. After loading we started south, encountering heavy winds and rainstorms most of the way. We arrived safe and sound and discharged the cargo and took on a cargo for London, England. The cargo consisted of hard pine and cotton seed in the hold and five hundred barrels of rosin on deck. While loading there the crew undertook to desert in the night, but the watchman on the wharf stopped them and notified the Captain, who had them all put in the calaboose until the vessel was loaded. After loading we went down stream and anchored, when a policeman brought the crew aboard.

After they were on board we asked them to turn to and man the vessel, and on their refusing to do so we put them all in irons and lashed them to a spar that was to the main hatch. The towboat's crew assisted us to make sail and towed us to sea. When the towboat dropped our line we squared away for London. About three hours after the towboat left the men concluded to turn to, as they could not help themselves. We had very heavy weather, making sail and taking it in most of the time, until we arrived off the banks of Newfoundland. After passing the banks we had a very heavy hurricane. We ran under a lown foretopsail and reefed foresail, and as the hurricane increased caused us to ship large quantities of water, which started our deck-load of rosin adrift, and we could not secure it, as the vessel rolled so and the heavy seas were continually breaking over us, and for fear it would start the vessel leaking the Captain ordered it thrown overboard. In order to lighten her as soon as possible the Captain took the wheel and I took the crew and began throwing the rosin overboard, breaking in some of them where we could, and where it was not so easy to break them in we rolled them over as they were.

We had thrown over the whole deck-load all but three barrels, when, in the middle of the night, we shipped a very heavy sea. We were running dead before the wind, when I saw a large sea coming astern. I jumped up on the house, calling to the crew at the same time to look out for themselves. I had but just got hold of the rigging when the sea broke clear over the stern of the vessel. We had a boat swung astern and the sea slammed it against the main boom, breaking it in two, and but for the boat being there the captain would have been instantly killed at the wheel, as the boat broke the force of the sea. Besides smashing our boat it stove in the cabin and started it from the deck and filled it more than half full of water. My wife was the only woman on board and the only occupant of the cabin at the time. And she, instead of fainting as many men would have done at such a time, grasped the lamp from a socket and held it up to the binnacle so the vessel could be kept in her course, as the binnacle was smashed, lamp and all.

Hers was not a very comfortable position, nearly waist deep in water holding up a lamp so the helmsman could see how to steer. That was a good sign of presence of mind in an emergency. She knew as soon as the binnacle light went out something must be done to give those on deck light, and acted as stated above; and she was more than praised for her bravery. While holding the light the second mate went below for a tackle to put on to the wheel or tiller, as the wheel was broken, and it was the only means of safety at such a time, and being in the night made it much worse, as it is not pleasant in a hurricane in a dark night. As he went below Mrs. Crapo asked him the extent of the damage, when he replied, "I shouldn't wonder if the whole stern is stove in." Her reply was, "Well, if that is the case we will not be here very long," when he made the remark that he didn't think we would last until morning. When my wife told me of the conversation I talked quite strongly to him for trying to frighten her. Provided he thought so, he should have tried to cheer her up, instead of scaring her at such a time; but he was, no doubt, as much or more frightened than she was.

We at last succeeded in getting a tackle on the tiller so we could handle her, and with a man to attend to it, with my wife still holding the lamp, I went forward and ordered the foresail clewed up, then the lower topsail, still holding her before the wind. We then hoisted and set one two-reefed mainsail with a winch. The captain then ordered me to try and save the pieces of the boat hanging alongside. I replied by trying to save it. We might have lost the vessel, so I ordered it cut away. We then put the rudder down to lay the vessel to, when she shipped another heavy sea, which washed the remaining three barrels of rosin from forward clear aft, and we soon launched them overboard. As soon as daylight broke we set to work repairing the wheel and cabin door and getting the water out of the cabin. We were all tired out and wet through, and what rest we got was by lying down where we could just as we were for a short time.

During the forenoon the lamp in my room, over my desk, was taken out of its socket by the steward and put on my desk, and the rolling of the vessel threw it off and into my bed, setting the clothes on fire. The captain happened to go below and saw it just in time to avoid a terrible catastrophe, and saved us all from a horrible fate. We continued to lay to until about four o'clock in the afternoon, when the wind moderated and the sea went down a little, so we could set a reefed foresail and lown topsail. We ran that way until the next morning, when we put on the upper topsail and ran that way until we sighted Land's End, England, when the weather moderated and all sail was set, and good weather prevailed the balance of the passage to London.

While discharging the cargo all of the crew, including the steward, deserted. After discharging our cargo we took on part of a load of cement for New York. We were there nearly a month, and when ready to sail the captain shipped four sailors and a steward. We then towed part way down the Thames river; we then made sail and beat down to the downs off Deals and came to an anchor. It blew very hard, so we dropped both anchors, as we were drifting. Two of the sailors that were shipped in London were no good at all and didn't seem to know anything; they shipped as able seamen, but were not near as good as ordinary seamen.

We remained at anchor about three days, when the second mate went forward to call the sailors to heave up anchors and make sail for a start, when the two that I said were no good refused to do so, saying they were sick, and the other two refused unless the captain would ship two more good men. The second mate came aft and told me what they said. I reported the case to the captain, who said, "Put them in irons." Right here I will say that there are a great many pretended sailors who work such tricks on captains of vessels, as they generally secure a good advance, and then form some scheme to get away from the vessel. On going forward with the handcuffs they refused to be put in irons, which I also reported to the captain. We then both went forward, when a scuffle ensued, one of them stabbing me with a knife in the back of my neck, which has left a large scar that I will carry to my grave. The thrust was meant to kill, as the knife went in all of two inches, and by placing my finger where it went makes a very funny feeling at the present time. A sheath knife is an ugly thing to be cut with.

We then hoisted our flag in the rigging union down, a sign of distress, when a boat came from shore to ascertain the cause of distress, and took the captain and myself on shore, where I was put in a hospital for treatment. I was there four days before my wife was allowed to see me, as my case was a critical one. The doctor thought I would not pull through, but with a good constitution I soon rallied. After I went to the hospital the police went on board the vessel and took the mutinous sailors on shore and lodged them in jail. While in the hospital the sailors were brought in and court was held there, and the decree of the court was that an American on an American vessel had no right to put a man in irons in English waters, a very queer ruling I thought for an attempt to murder, so the sailors were allowed to go free. I remained in the hospital about twelve days. After the men were set free the captain went to London and shipped four more men and a mate and sent the two that were playing sick on shore, as they were of no account at all. When the captain told me that he had shipped a mate to take my place it made me very indignant, and I refused to go with him, but he cried and took on so that at last I consented to go. I didn't like the idea at all, but he meant well and did so to make it easy for me as I was not able (yet I thought I was) to stand watch day and night, as I had not recovered from my wound, as it was such a deep cut it took a long time to heal, and it was a very close shave and a great wonder it did not sever my jugular vein or my backbone.

The hospital surgeon gave me permission to go, but told me I must be very careful, as I was not near out of danger yet, and told me not to undertake to do anything but to keep as quiet as possible. After going on board at daylight we hove up anchor and made sail for our journey to New York. We had very good weather the first part of the passage, and it was about twenty days before my neck healed. I had an easy time of it as my regular duties fell upon the new mate, and I let him fill the position without molestation on my part. On the latter part of the passage we had very heavy weather, but fortunately did not carry away anything, either sails or rigging, and at last arrived off Sandy Hook. The captain then gave me all orders instead of the new mate, and as we took a towboat we were soon at the wharf in New York. As soon as we were made fast the captain discharged the whole crew, mate and all. After discharging the cargo, Captain Nash went home to Harrington, Maine, and sent on a Captain Roberts to command her in his place. After he arrived we chartered to load coal at Port Johnson, New Jersey, for Salem, Mass.

After we finished loading we shipped a second mate and four sailors and a steward. We towed to Port Johnson, a distance of about four miles. Our cargo consisted of about five hundred and fifty tons. We again hired a towboat and towed through Hurl Gate. After the towboat cast off our lines we set our sails and headed down Long Island sound towards our destination. We had a very pleasant run all the way. On arriving at Salem we were fortunate in discharging below the bridge, as vessels heavily laden many times have hard work in getting up to the wharves above the bridge, and they must catch the tide at its full, as at low water the water about all flows out, and if a vessel gets caught above on her way to the wharf when the tide is going out she remains in the thick mud, when at extreme low water there is scarcely water enough for a duck to swim in. Many times a towboat will start with a loaded vessel and probably get about half way to the wharf when the muddy water soon tells them they had better let go and get into deep water themselves or else they will have to lie in the mud.

By being left in the mud quite a distance from the wharf means hard work for the sailors, because as soon as it is high water one must take the boat and scull with a line from one side to the other while those on board haul her along until she is made fast. So I considered ourselves very fortunate in discharging below the bridge. As soon as we were made fast to the wharf the captain discharged all hands but myself, and made a visit to his home while I superintended the discharging and taking in ballast. When he arrived I concluded to leave the vessel, so my wife and I took the train for New Bedford. I remained at home a short time and then started into the fish business, but I did not succeed very well, so I sold out and gave it up. I then hired out to work in a junk store, where I remained a few months, but it was not agreeable to me as I was not used to working on shore.

I had for years been thinking about crossing the Atlantic Ocean in a small boat, in fact I was very anxious to outstrip any attempt that had ever been made. Anyone would naturally think that knowing what the ocean was by living

on it so many years would banish all thoughts of any such
attempt, but not so with me. I was venturesome and
daring and I thought if I could manage to eclipse all
others I could make considerable money by so doing. I
knew it would be a daring feat, had it not been I don't
think I would have pondered over it as much as I did.
The more I thought of it the more decided and determined
I became.

While working in the junk store, unbeknown to everybody but my wife, I perfected my plans of a boat that I
considered capable of crossing from this country to England in. After looking over my plans very carefully for
several days I considered them perfect in every particular.
I formed them partially on the plan of a whaleboat, as
they were the most seaworthy of any kind ever built; in
fact they could hardly be improved upon. But as I should
have to live right in her I had to form my plans accordingly. After satisfying myself that everything was as I
wanted it, I took my plans to a boat-builder named Samuel
Mitchell, on Fish Island, in the Acushnet river, adjoining
New Bedford, by a bridge. He had become famous as a
whaleboat builder, and for that reason, coupled with my
acquaintance with him, I employed him to build my boat
exactly as I had planned her.

I do not remember whether any conversation ever passed
between us in regard to what use I intended to put her to
or not, as I was very careful not to speak of it to anyone,
even to my employers and fellow workmen. She was completed about the tenth of May, 1877, so I removed her
from his shop and stowed her away for a few days. On
the following Saturday night I informed my employers
that I did not intend to work for them any longer, when,
as was natural, they asked my reasons for leaving them,
and I told them I was going to sea again. I did not tell

them that I was going in my dory boat, but the following day, Sunday, they and nearly everybody else in New Bedford heard of it, and a desire to see the boat took possession of everybody. Everybody had something to talk about, so it was as well, or better, advertised than if it had been published in the newspapers.

It was the topic of the day, and many shook their heads as much as to say, he must be crazy; but whether I was considered so or not, the object of my desire for years was about to be tested, and nothing could change my mind. As I, like all sailors, had spent my earnings as fast as I made them, I wanted to get a little ahead for a rainy day, and I thought if I could only succeed I could exhibit the boat and myself, and by charging a small fee for admission I could make a little money. The ocean had never been crossed in so small a craft, and has not since, as mine was the only one of her size that, to my knowledge, ever made the attempt.

My intentions were to go from New Bedford, Massachusetts, to England, and the most important feature of the trip was that, owing to the boat being so small, I could not carry a chronometer, so the voyage must be made by dead reckoning, depending on passing vessels to furnish me with my position, as the captains always know just what latitude and longitude they are in, and about the distance from port, so my readers can see what a seemingly rash undertaking I was about; yet I was confident of success, and never for a moment doubted my reaching England in safety. I was positive my little boat could live where a large vessel could, and I scanned her with a longing akin to love, as a good boat is a sailor's paradise.

CHAPTER IV.

ACROSS THE ATLANTIC OCEAN IN A DORY BOAT.

As I began to make preparations to rig my boat with her masts and sails, my wife was all anxiety about my intended trip, and the idea preyed on her mind until at last she informed me that if I went she should go too. This was something I had not thought of for a moment; and, again, how could two go with such a small craft, with hardly room for one and turn around? But there I was, face to it, and I knew my wife's courage, as I had seen it tested, and I knew, without argument, that when she said she was going she meant it, and that settled it. There was no use trying to dissuade her, as it would only be wasting breath, so I took the matter as coolly as possible. Had I known things would have taken such a turn I would have had my boat built a trifle larger on her account; but it could not be done now, as she was all built.

My readers can see how cramped we would be for room, as I had the boat built just nineteen feet and seven inches long, six feet and two inches wide, and thirty inches deep, and she only drew thirteen inches of water, with us and everything on board. Her foremast was twenty-one and one-half feet long, and the mainmast was twenty and one-half feet long. Her main boom was about ten feet long, the foresail contained fifteen yards of light duck, and the mainsail ten yards. Just twenty-five yards of sail to carry two people across the Atlantic Ocean! Just think of it! Her measurements were one ton and sixty-two one-hundredths of a ton, her actual weight being about five hundred pounds. She was decked over on top, and had two scuttles, one forward and one aft. The one aft I had to sit in to steer, so my readers can see plainly what a large amount of room we had to eat, drink and sleep in. It was a vast difference between our limited accommodations and the comforts of a palatial steamer to cross to England.

I rigged her as I intended, and had her photographed on Fish Island before launching her; the accompanying picture below shows her exactly as she looked with myself and wife on board. I then launched her, and the following Monday put my kegs which were to contain fresh water for drinking purposes on board in position, and again she was photographed. I gave it out that I with my wife would start on the 28th of that month (May). My intentions were to have a trial trip in her, but I did not get a chance. I kept her moored at Fish Island, and the following Sunday the Reverend James Butler, of the Seamen's Bethel, held religious services on the Island, which were largely attended, as it looked as though the whole city had turned out.

The next day I put on board our provisions, which consisted of ninety pounds of biscuits, seventy-five pounds of canned meats, and one hundred gallons of fresh water for drinking purposes and for making tea or coffee. We also carried a sufficient quantity of tea, coffee, sugar and other light articles. The two scuttles I mentioned were eighteen by twenty-four inches in size, and the one where Captain Crapo would sit to steer was to be used for a dining table (meaning, of course, the sliding cover).

The report of our intended voyage spread like wildfire, and the papers everywhere published more or less in regard to it, and I will give my readers the benefit of one which appeared in the New York Times which read as follows:

"It is reported that a New Bedford sea captain has started with his wife on a very perilous expedition. He has undertaken to cross the Atlantic in a small boat of two tons burden and measuring about twenty feet, and of course he has been called a bold and reckless man by all the papers which have written on the subject. That this is a correct estimate of his character the New York Times feels more than assured."

These words the Journal thinks hardly do justice to his courage; though this is not so much shown, the writer imagines, in the fact of his attempting to cross the ocean in a small boat as in his taking his wife with him on so long and lonely a voyage. Very few husbands and wives have been in each other's company or society without rest or intermission for forty days, and the New York Times does not believe that this can be made to answer.

When nature placed men's offices in town and their homes in the suburbs she made provision for temporary separations which are absolutely necessary. Married people living on shore can always escape from each other's society on certain occasions when escape seems desirable, but in a small boat this is out of the question. When, goaded by the refusal of the galley fire to burn, she begins an exhaustive analysis of the captain's character and gradually shows that he is a brutal and loathsome tyrant, he will be compelled to listen.

There is not a nook or corner of the boat to which the clear tones of an earnest woman will not penetrate. When in his turn he finds the coffee somewhat cold, and thereupon expresses with all the resources of forcible language at the command of an experienced sailor, the conviction that there is no crime, from murder up to frying beefsteak, of which she is not capable, she must either listen or jump overboard.

At first all may go well, that is to say, very much at first —quite at the beginning of the voyage. Perhaps for the first two days they may be happy; but about the third day the writer is afraid that a sunburnt nose does not add to his wife's attractiveness, and she, on her part, will ask herself if it is possible for a woman to respect a man who uses tobacco. Such little differences will surely arise, and the remedy of a temporary separation being impossible, a week —but a small portion of the forty days the voyage is to take if all goes well—will probably land them in the middle of a considerable " row."

The New York Times therefore predicts that the journey will not be made, and pictures the travelers returning to the starting place, after a short absence, when the husband will spring to land and make straight for Siberia by the shortest route; and the wife will rush to torrid zones with at least equal rapidity, after, perhaps, having had one final claw at the departing mariner.

As the greater portion of our food was cooked and in cans, we merely had to warm it up when required to serve. As cooking to any extent would be entirely out of the question, as our stove was a small kerosene lamp stove made to hold a pint of oil, so my readers can plainly see what disadvantages we were about to undergo, but our accommodations were limited, so of course we had to get along the best we could. And again, we were more or less afraid of an explosion, as the boat, in heavy weather especially, would jump and roll about so as to make it unsafe to put much oil in at a time, so we never put in more than a gill at any time.

This being the day set for sailing, we had to hurry in order to make our start without disappointing the multitude of people collected on the wharves and vessels, and especially in row and sailboats, which were very numerous. In fact, I never before or since saw so many boats on the river on any occasion. And as it had been published in the papers, many people came on the noon train to see us. Ladies, especially, would force themselves through the crowd in order to get near enough to shake hands with my wife, and many there were more than surprised to see the miniature boat we were going in. Surprise and wonder could be seen pictured on their faces, and no doubt a great many of them were saying to themselves, they will not go far on that little boat and will soon be back again, the laughing stock of the community. The most noticeable of all at this time was an old lady that I think arrived on the train who forced her way to the side of my wife. Her gray hair denoted the passing of many summers and as many dreary winters. She shook the hand of my wife in a very affectionate manner, saying : "My dear child, are you not afraid to trust yourself in such a small boat, on such a dangerous undertaking? You are young and very brave, and I earnestly hope you will merit what you deserve."

My old father was as near us and our boat as he could possibly get, crying and wringing his hands in a manner pitiful to see in an old man of his years, and constantly saying, "The two foolish children, I shall never see them again." All this time I was getting our things on board, and as it was nearing our time of starting I did not have time to stow things as they should be. My drogue, line and anchor, compass and water kegs and many other smaller articles were presented to me by friends. Many of my wife's friends were trying to persuade her from making the attempt, but to no avail. She was as determined as I was. All this time the crowd was growing larger, as many quit work to see us off.

At last I was ready to cast off, and was about to do so when Captain Humphrey Seabury of New Bedford, a well known and respected citizen, appeared and presented me with a compass that had probably been used on more than one whaleship, and was a reliable one at all times, and I was more than pleased to receive it. He also gave me two charts and an old fashioned square lantern, the fore side of glass fitted to slide out when necessary to clean. It was fitted to burn candles in, and he also gave me a quantity of candles to burn in it. He, being an old sea captain, knew what would be the most essential at such a time, and I was very thankful to him for them. As soon as I cast off our line a general hurrah was given and handkerchiefs were waving everywhere. The yachts at their moorings fired a salute as we passed and many boats sailed down the bay in company with us, the boats in the harbor being so thick as to make it almost impossible to get through, and all of them wanted to keep as near to us as they possibly could.

As my boat was so small the Custom House officials could not issue marine documents to me, so I carried the following letter :—

CUSTOM HOUSE, NEW BEDFORD, MASS.
COLLECTOR'S OFFICE, May 28th, 1877.

Captain Thomas Crapo and his wife, both of this city, being about to sail from this port in a boat called the " New Bedford," measuring 1$\frac{62}{100}$ tons, bound for London, England, requests me to give him a letter, as, on account of the small size of his vessel, I cannot issue " marine documents."

I, therefore, desire to make it known to " all whom it may concern " that Captain Crapo is well known here, and his purpose is entirely legitimate, and he has the good wishes of this community that his voyage may be successfully accomplished.

J. A. P. ALLEN,
Collector of Customs.

As we had hurriedly put our things on board they were not stowed as we intended to have them, as at present they were all in a heap. While we must make some preparations for trimming the boat I found I should have to anchor or run in to some port, and as I perceived she was leaking considerable on account of not having been in the water long enough to swell her tight, I decided to run in at Vineyard Haven for the night. In crossing the bay the wind blew quite fresh from the southwest and the boat behaved very creditably. As we arrived off Woods Holl the wharves everywhere were black with people, as telegrams had been sent to them to be on the lookout for us, and cheer upon cheer rent the air while hats and handkerchiefs were waving from every available point.

We continued on to Vineyard Haven and ran up along-side of the wharf, when I found that the boat had leaked more than a foot of water, and had wet our bedding and other things. A very enthusiastic crowd of people met us and gave us a hearty welcome. It was about six o'clock in the afternoon when we arrived, and as night was fast approaching and I wanted to get away as soon as possible I began taking the things out to dry, and after they were removed I had a tin pump made to pump her out with. We also disposed of a large quantity of photographs of the boat with ourselves on board. We were also invited to go to the hotel called the Mansion House, which invitation we gratefully accepted, especially as it was tendered to us as a compliment by the people of Vineyard Haven.

After we arrived we had tea and adjourned to the hotel parlors, where we were asked all sorts of questions relative to our intended trip. We retired early in order to get as much sleep as possible, as it would probably be a long time, if ever, before we would again sleep in a nice comfortable bed. We arose about daylight, and after partaking of a breakfast we walked down towards our little boat, followed by a very eager throng of people. On arriving we found that many of our things were still damp, so we waited for them to dry. About nine o'clock I found that our things were about dry, so we put them on board again, and was about to cast off, when the Reverend L. R. Wait, of Vineyard Haven, delivered a short speech, and at the close of his remarks he handed my wife a letter, telling her to open it at sea.

This was on the twenty-ninth of May, 1877. We then cast off our lines and hoisted our sails, amid cheers from the crowd assembled on the wharf. The wind was from the southward and westward, and was blowing quite fresh. Handkerchiefs and hats continued to wave nearly as long as we could see the wharf. Quite a fleet of vessels were at anchor in the harbor, the crews of which also cheered us lustily as we passed them. We headed direct towards Chatham, on Cape Cod, by crossing Vineyard Sound close in towards the north shore. We had comparatively calm water. Our colors flying informed the people on shore who we were, and those that did see us cheered as we passed by them. Our leg of mutton sails were, no doubt, a strange sight to many, as none of that make are used around here or there; but they are used extensively by the inhabitants of islands in mid-ocean, as they hold the wind below, instead of aloft, therefore they are considered far safer.

The report of our coming seemed to have preceded us, as on our arrival, about four o'clock in the afternoon, we were met by a multitude of people. When running in we struck several times on sand bars, but did not do any damage to our boat. As we stepped on shore we were surrounded by a large number of inquiring people, that asked all manner of questions relative to our intended trip across the Atlantic. We could only answer them civilly, and Captain Darius Hammond extended an invitation to us to make his home ours during our stay, which must be short, at best, as we were anxious to be on our way. We accepted this kind invitation in the same spirit as it was tendered, and then proceeded to his home, but a short distance away.

88

The next morning the captain and myself went around
to find a carpenter, as I wanted to make a few alterations
to my boat. The two scuttles which I spoke of in the
first part of this adventure were cut out eighteen by
twenty-four inches, and the top was rather too low to suit
us, as we wanted them somewhat higher and fitted so they
would slide. We were at last fortunate in finding a man
that could do it at once, so he set to work and put comb-
ings around each, and fitted them as we wanted them.
After this was completed I also had two hundred pounds
of iron put in for ballast, as what we had was not sufficient
to keep her steady. After this was completed, I had a
painter to paint her a good thick coat, to make her water-
tight, if possible, as I did not care about having too much
water inside, as we did not have any room for it, and it
was not to our liking, as there would be plenty all around
us, in case we needed it for anything.

Repairs and painting were finished on the first of June,
and the next day, June 2d, at two o'clock in the afternoon,
we hove up our anchor, and as we would have to proceed
through a very narrow passage, a man volunteered to tow
us out with his dory. The crowd on shore gave three
rousing cheers as we started, and hats and handkerchiefs
were waving all along the shore. We carried from there
two letters that were handed to us by a Captain Taylor
(whose son was in Liverpool, England), who requested me
to mail them as soon as we landed.

On arriving in deep water, our pilot left us, with our
thanks for his favor, and we then squared off for our destination, England. From this time until our arrival we were
to undergo what we had never dreamed of. Just imagine
to yourself what it would be in pleasant weather, to be
several miles out of sight of land, in a small boat, just for
one day and night. You would think it the longest night

you had ever seen. Yet here we were, sailing across the boundless waste of waters, all the time going farther and farther away, and whatever the weather should be,—rain, thunder and lightning, or a heavy gale of wind,—we would have to grin and take it as it came; the thought was not very inviting, to say the least.

We started on our course with a moderate south wind, and a comparatively smooth sea. Land faded from our view about five o'clock, and the sun soon began to draw close to the horizon, which plainly told us that night was fast approaching. At last it sank below the surface, and darkness soon settled over us. I found it hard work to keep awake, but I knew that I must exert myself to do so. Mrs. Crapo retired early, which left me alone with nothing but water in sight. The wind was blowing about what is called a three knot breeze, and the little boat skimmed over the surface of the water like a duck. Mrs. Crapo's apartments were not large enough for her to lose herself in when she lay down to sleep. Her feet rested on the water kegs, and should she desire to turn over she would first have to rise; so my readers can form an idea what limited accommodations we were subjected to, and must put up with for a considerable length of time.

At last signs of daylight appeared, and as the black pall of night was lifted nothing but a dreary waste of water could be seen on every hand. Soon the welcome voice of my partner, bidding me good morning, was heard, which was pleasant to hear at such a time. Soon the glorious orb of day rose in all its majestic splendor, and it was a pretty sight to see bright rays along the water glistening and sparkling like burnished gold.

We soon began preparations for our first breakfast. Mrs. Crapo put a gill of oil in our lamp stove, and lighted it, preparatory to making coffee. She then unearthed our monster coffeepot, which, when full, held but a pint, and very soon the pleasant aroma of boiling coffee greeted our nostrils, and it made us hungry to think of it. My appetite was somewhat sharpened, and as soon as all was in readiness I was ready to do justice to it by eating a good hearty meal; and we both felt in better trim to endure whatever it was our lot to face, as nothing excels a full stomach on any occasion, especially as we were alone, and as you may say had nothing to do but eat, drink and sleep. Yet I had to steer the boat as straight towards our destination as possible, at all times; even while eating I kept her on her course.

I wish further to inform my readers how we had to make our coffee. As the motion of the boat rendered it unsafe to leave a lighted lamp stove anywhere unattended, my wife placed it between my feet, so the motion of the boat would not have any effect upon it, as no one knows when they will explode. It would, I am sure, make a person laugh to see us preparing our meals; but it was our only source, as our kitchen, pantry, sitting-room, dining-room, and parlor, were all connected, and it did not take us long to go to any part of the house. Should my wife be reading in the sitting-room or parlor, I could summon her at any time by merely whispering, so we had no use for speaking tubes.

After we had finished our morning meal, the utensils for preparing it were again put away, and we passed the long hours of the morning (we did not expect any callers so did not put ourselves out any in making any useless preparations) in relating little incidents connected with our attempted voyage. Thus the day wore on, and as the only reading matter we had with us was a Bible and a few tracts, we had to converse on different subjects, as the time began to hang heavy as the sun passed over our heads.

This being the third of June, and about four o'clock in the afternoon, I concluded to heave the boat to and have a short nap, as I had steered from our starting the day previous, making a total of twenty-six consecutive hours without rest, and tired nature began to assert her rights. So I lowered the foresail and hauled aft the main sheet, and then curled myself up for a snooze, and it did not take me long to pass the portals of sweet sleep, as I was very tired, as there was not much chance to move my limbs while steering.

While I was sleeping the vessel was in charge of my mate, who had proven herself to be an accomplished sailor. I slept until about eight o'clock, when I hoisted my foresail and slacked off my main sheet and again headed for England, the land of roses, which lay about east by north from us. The weather continued to be fair but the nights were very chilly. My mate again retired early, which left me monarch of all I surveyed, and with a good four knot breeze we went skimming along, the only thing to break the monotony was the noise of the boat cutting through the water. I eagerly watched for signs of daylight, as I knew that a cup of good hot coffee would not only refresh but drive the chilly, numb feeling away. As I sat cramped all up in such a small space so long it was a luxury to get a chance to stretch my legs and arms.

At last the morning of June fourth greeted us with a four knot wind and water about the same as on the preceding day. On casting our eyes about we sighted a number of fishing vessels anchored on what is called the "George's Banks." We ran up to one, which proved to be the schooner A. J. Chapman, of New London, Conn., fishing for halibut. The crew at the time were absent in the dories attending to their trawls, so the captain was the only one we saw on board. He asked us where we were bound

and numerous other questions.   He also coaxed us to come
on board and get a cup of good hot coffee, but as we had
just had some we respectfully declined the invitation with
thanks.   He then proposed for us to come on board and
stretch our limbs, but this we also declined.   So we bade
him good-bye and sailed on our course.

In the afternoon we sighted two vessels on the wind
making to the southward and westward and about four
miles from us.   About four o'clock in the afternoon I
again hove the boat to and took another nap until eight in
the evening, which made another twenty hours of steering
without rest.   About this time my wife began to feel a
little qualmish, as the motion of the boat was considerable
quicker than a large vessel, and as the boat had begun
to dance considerably it had the above-mentioned effect
on her.

The following was taken from a New York paper and
printed in the New Bedford Standard, which was mailed
to me in England:

THE "NEW BEDFORD."

Fishing schooner A. J. Chapman, which arrived at New
York, from George's Banks, Wednesday, reports speaking
the New Bedford June fourth, lat. 41.55, lon. 67.10.
Captain Crapo and wife were well.   This, however, was
two or three days previous to the date the New Bedford
was spoken, which was before reported.

When I awoke we again made sail and sailed on our
course, and as my wife was getting quite nervous she remained up instead of going to bed.   She kept me company
until nearly daylight, when tired nature gave way and she
lay down to sleep, and after a short time I hove the boat to
and took a nap myself.   The wind still held to the westward and the sea was quite calm.   This was on the fifth

of June, our third day from Chatham. We sailed along
all day without seeing anything more than gulls and porpoises, which were quite numerous. Again another night
closed in and the ripple of the water against the boat was
all there was to break the monotony. As Mrs. Crapo remained awake it made the time pass more pleasantly, as
the nights seemed very long. The next day, June the
sixth, the sun arose in all its splendor. It was a pleasing
sight to watch it rise, seemingly from out the ocean, and
soar aloft to cast its pleasant rays on land and sea. As
there was no sail in sight I again hove the boat to and took
a nap until about eight o'clock when I again made sail and
proceeded on our course. We saw a great many storm
petrel, better known as Mother Carey's chickens. After
we had got well under way we decided to open the letter
handed to us at Vineyard Haven, which we were to open
and read at sea. We broke the seal and on opening it the
following met our eyes:

VINEYARD HAVEN, May 29th, 1877.

Brother and Sister Crapo:—When you are at sea remember you have the prayers of millions to cheer you on
your perilous journey. We commend you to the God who
watches over you on sea as well as on the land. Commit
your ways to Him and be calm in times of danger. You
go with the good wishes of many.

Yours in good feeling,

LYMAN R. WAIT, Minister.

This was encouraging, indeed, to think that, away from
the bustle of the busy world, alone on the broad expanse
of water many miles away from home and friends, these
kind words were felt with an intense longing to shake the
hands of those who would eagerly watch for reports from
us from time to time, yet could they but realize what we

must endure before reaching the goal we so eagerly sought their anxiety would be far greater for our safety. As many, many times large vessels go to sea and are never heard from again, either burned at sea or wrecked in a gale. And for us two persons to venture in such a frail craft was what set the millions of people to wondering what the result would be. So we talked over that letter for quite a length of time, as it was a good subject for us; thus the day passed and night again spread her mantle over the world.

We did not mind the voyage by daylight but after night set in it was far from pleasant, as in the daylight we could see whatever was within reach of our sight, but darkness hid everything; and it is very surprising, when we realize what quantities of grampus, porpoise, blackfish, school killers, whales, and other large monsters there are in the ocean, that we were not smashed in pieces in the night or that none of them came up to the surface under our boat, which as they cannot breathe under water they come to the surface to do so. Yet we are pleased to say nothing of the kind happened, and we earnestly hoped the balance of our perilous journey would be as safe for us. At last the long night passed and daylight was upon us. After my usual nap we again proceeded on our journey. This being the seventh of June made it our fifth day at sea.

My wife began to feel decidedly better, as she had now got used to the motion of the boat, which made it far pleasanter for both of us. Nothing appeared in sight at daylight, or when I awoke from my usual nap, and after we had partaken of our breakfast we continued on, with a four-knot breeze from the southwest. About one o'clock in the afternoon we sighted a sail, and as it appeared to be coming our way we continued on our course, and very soon we could see her hull very plainly. She continued to

draw closer, so we headed for her, and as we drew close
up with her I spoke her. She proved to be the ship Gustave and Oscar, from Bremen, bound to New York. After
informing the captain of our intended voyage, I asked
him what our position was. He informed us that we were
about two hundred miles due south from Liverpool, Nova
Scotia. We requested him to report us, which he prom-
ised to do; and below, kind reader, you will find the
report he gave, which was printed in a New York paper.
We then parted company, receiving hearty cheers from the
crew, and the ship's colors were dipped to us as a parting
salute, and as we were sailing in opposite directions it was
not long before she was entirely out of sight.

The report of the ship Gustave and Oscar, which was.
printed, as the reader will readily see, before the A. J.
Chapman arrived in port; therefore, although the Chapman spoke us first, her report was given to the world after
the one below, which read as follows, which was copied
exact from the papers now in my possession :

"THE NEW BEDFORD SPOKEN FIVE DAYS OUT."

New York, June 10th. The ship Gustave and Oscar,
from Bremen, reports that on June 7th, latitude 42.20,
longitude 64.22, spoke small two-masted boat from New
Bedford for London, having one man and woman on board,
undoubtedly Captain Crapo and his wife. Crapo's position
when spoken was at a point nearly due south from Liverpool, Nova Scotia, and almost due east from Boston.
Chatham, from whence he made his last start, is in longitude 70, consequently he had, up to the time he was
spoken, in longitude 64.22, sailed five degrees and thirty-
eight minutes, or about 5 2-3 degrees. Falmouth, England, where Mr. Crapo intends stopping, is in about
longitude 5, and the whole distance across in a straight

line from Chatham is about 65 degrees. The length of a degree of longitude in latitude 42 is 51 1-4 miles, consequently the New Bedford had sailed when spoken, a little over 290 miles from Chatham, out of the 3,300 and over which she must sail before reaching Falmouth.

So my readers can more fully understand by this report just what our situation was when spoken, and although we had been sailing along most of the time for five days when spoken we had only covered a very small distance, comparatively. Yet we were in good spirits, and had not at this time encountered any serious weather, yet we were liable to at any time.

Shortly after she disappeared night again spread her mantle over us. The wind died down and left the sea in a dead calm, and to make things more uninviting, a thick fog set in, which made us very uncomfortable; as my readers can imagine what a cold, damp fog in the night is, especially out at sea in a small boat. About nine o'clock we were given a surprise party, which at that time was not received with much enthusiasm, as we were put to considerable inconvenience, both in mind and body, the participants being a large school of sperm whales, which forced their company upon us uninvited.

This was a bad predicament to be in, as sperm whales are very dangerous at all times; and if one of them should by chance touch our boat he would slash it into fragments with his flukes. They have very small eyes, and as they are quite a distance back from the end of the head, they can only see on each side of them; so my readers can just imagine one of them swimming along, with his large flat nose bunting into our little boat, which would undoubtedly have tipped her over and left us to the mercy of the whales and sea.

My wife was very much frightened, and she was not to

blame for being so, as our position was rather precarious. She asked me if there was any danger, and of course I did not want to make her any worse by telling her just what danger we were in. She wanted me to shoot them, or anything to drive them away; and as a splash in the water or a strange noise will sometimes scare them off, I decided to try to get rid of them, as many times they came so close that the vapor they blow out, which is their breath, would blow over us and the boat, like steam from the spout of a teakettle, so I made a noise with my rudder which soon had the desired effect. My fear was that in sounding one of them might rise to the surface under the boat, in case of which our fate would never have been known, as we would have been thrashed to pieces in their fury. And we were both easier in mind when they left us, and we surely did not extend to them an invitation to call again, as they had forced their company upon us for nearly seven hours, which had caused us to dislike them very much, and their continued puffing was not a pleasing sound in our ears as there was not much music to it, their voices not being properly cultivated.

We looked for their reappearance until daylight, and were pleased to be disappointed. The fog still hung heavy around us and a light breeze sprang up from the southeast, and as the whales were not to be seen or heard, I took my usual nap. This was on June 8th. When I awoke we had our breakfast and pulled in our drogue and squared away on our course. Everything went well considering the thick fog, which kept us busy listening for the fog horns of passing vessels. I had used mine until it was played out and practically useless, which made us more on the alert as we were in danger of being run down, as we could only use our lungs, providing we heard a vessel's warning of her approach.

Early in the afternoon it began to rain very hard. This was more than we wished for as I was drenched to the skin, and to sit all cramped up and keep her on her course was not very pleasant at best. One does not dread a rain storm on shore, as by bundling up and with an umbrella they can get along very comfortably, but I could do neither, as I had to sit still and let the rain beat on my unprotected body as it pleased. I was not afraid of taking cold, as that is a very unusual thing at sea, yet in years to come it is liable to cause rheumatism. This being on the 9th of June, coupled with our trials with the whales and the first heavy rainstorm, made the date impressed very strongly on our memory. Towards night the rain ceased, but the fog still hung on and darkness soon settled around us. Another tedious night was upon us.

June 10th was ushered in with the fog still holding on as though it meant to watch over us at all times, and seemed to like our company far more than we wished it did. We heard the fog signals of two vessels but could not see them on account of the thick fog that encircled us. At times it would light up a little and then shut in as before and we had to keep our eyes and ears on the alert at all times, as we were in the track of vessels sailing to and from the United States. Thus the day passed and again night settled around us.

June 11th opened with the fog still holding its own, and a moderate breeze. The same continued through the 12th and 13th. The morning of the 14th opened with a heavy wind from the southwest. The wind increased so much that during the afternoon I hove to and put out my drogue to steady her. The seas ran mountains high, and I soon found that my drogue was insufficient to hold the boat steady, it being too light. Oh, how I wished I had something to make a heavier one, but I did not have the necessary articles to do so, so I must make it answer in some way.

We laid to until daylight of the 15th, when the wind moderated and we again started on our course. On figuring up by dead reckoning I found we were in lat. 43.46, lon. 58.54. During the day we were again surrounded by a school of whales, and I found it hard work to steer clear from them. Again night spread her mantle over us, and with the fog still holding on we passed the dreary night. In the early morning I took a nap, the first sleep I had had for twenty-four hours. As we were having more or less heavy weather regular meals were out of the question, so we ate whenever we chose. This was June 16th. We sailed along until about eight o'clock in the evening, when we hove to under our drogue and took cat naps through the night, at all times realizing our danger on account of the thick fog, yet the night passed without accident.

The next morning, about seven o'clock, the wind had moderated, so we took in our drogue and set sail for a start on our course, east by south. We were now in lat. 43.40 lon. 56.25. This was on the seventeenth. With a fresh breeze we sailed along. The wind was from the south west and began to increase until, at last, I furled the mainsail, and about one in the afternoon I had to furl the foresail and heave to with my drogue out to steady her. The wind kept increasing and the seas ran mountains high. It is impossible for me to try to picture to those unacquainted with the sea what a heavy gale is, as large ships are tossed about like chips and many times are lost, with all on board. So my readers can form a little idea what a position we were in in our little cockleshell of a boat, but we rode out the gale at last.

As we again hauled in our drogue about eleven o'clock

on the morning of June 18th, we again set sail and proceeded on our course, before the wind. The seas were
running so heavy that the boat labored very hard, and it
often looked as though we would be swamped; as the high
seas came up behind us it looked as though it would completely envelop us from sight. When in the trough of the
sea it looked like a large wall in front and back with no
chance of escape, but we would rise on top again like a
duck and shoot ahead ready to surmount the next one. By
dead reckoning we were in lat. 43.43, lon. 55.30.

Thus we sailed during the day and night, and the morning of the 19th opened with the wind considerably lighter
from the northwest and quite clear, and by four o'clock in
the afternoon it was very calm. We were now in lat. 43.32,
lon. 54.50. The wind increased again towards night and
before morning was again blowing a heavy gale.

The 20th was ushered in with the wind still increasing
and blowing from the south and a heavy rain set in. I
managed to catch a small pitcher full, while laid to under
our drogue. Late in the day the wind took a slant to the
west and moderated, when we again started, steering east-
southeast by the compass. The wind again increased, so
I furled the mainsail and ran before the wind under the
foresail with a heavy sea running from the west. I
had occasion to go forward, and when I returned I acci-
dentally stepped on my compass and broke the glass, but
did not do any other damage to it. I then took two of the
glasses from my lantern and fitted it the best I could, as
the small one I had was no good at all.

June 21st opened with a heavy gale from the westward.
We ran under foresail, and about two in the afternoon we
sighted a fisherman at anchor with a storm trysail up, as
the sea was running very heavy, on the Grand Banks
(Banks of Newfoundland). We were then running under

our foresail so we ran down and spoke her, and on inquiry we were informed that we were in lat. 43.43. The vessel proved to be a fisherman from Provincetown, but as she had so many boats around her we could not get her name. It was about three o'clock in the afternoon when we spoke her. We ran by and hove to in sight of her with our drogue out ahead. About five in the afternoon, while under our drogue, an English barque named the Amenori ran down and spoke us. She was from Baltimore, bound for Glasgow, Scotland. The captain asked if we wanted any assistance, and as we replied in the negative they proceeded after giving us the longitude, 50.1. As they passed they gave us a rousing cheer, and cries of good luck to you.

During the evening the wind moderated, but after midnight, during the early morning hours of the 22nd, it again increased, harder than before. I took in my mainsail and scudded under my foresail. I did not want to stop again if I could help it as I had just got under way, as the wind increased again and it was considerable work to keep putting out the drogue, but as the wind still kept increasing and the seas ran so high I had to heave to in order to insure our safety, and as everything appeared in good shape I took a short nap. As the gale continued I had a good time to rest, which I needed very much. During the time I figured by dead reckoning and found we were in lat. 43.54. I did not take the longitude every day. About five o'clock in the afternoon the wind took a lull and the sea quieted down a little, so I hauled in my drogue and squared away under our foresail; continued under the foresail through the night with the wind from the westward.

The 23rd was ushered in with a fresh breeze from the south, and it continued to increase. As we were sailing along with the wind on our beam we nearly capsized, and as I saw it would probably prove dangerous to continue I hove to under the drogue. Soon a heavy tempest set in and continued with very heavy rain nearly all night. My readers all know what a heavy thunderstorm is on shore, but it is nothing compared to a thunderstorm at sea; the sky settles as black as ink, when the thunder fairly shakes one's whole being and flashes of lightning nearly blind you. Simple words cannot adequately describe it. Every flash that dashes across the blackened heavens is plainly seen as there is nothing above the surface to break off the view, and the constant roll of the thunder, coupled with the drenching rain, was enough to make the strongest man quail.

Thunderstorms, as everybody knows, are never very pleasant, as they are almost always coupled with more or less danger. Many times the lightning strikes houses, trees, or human beings, and for us two to be alone in a little boat hundreds of miles from land and nothing but water in sight no wonder we were more or less frightened, and we were more than pleased when it passed over, as I was as wet as a drowned rat and had to keep a sharp lookout for fear of being run down by some ocean steamer or sailing vessel.

As I before stated, the drogue I had was far from being heavy enough to hold the boat steady, and really I class it as an interposition of Providence as I chanced to see a keg floating towards us, which I lost no time in securing, when I knocked the hoops off and cut them off with a hatchet, leaving them about fifteen inches in diameter. I then put three of them together and fastened them with rope yarns. I then took an old canvas hammock I had on board and cut it in the shape of a draw water bucket and sewed it to the hoops with rope yarns. I then fastened it with spun yarn so it would pull even, about the same as a bail to a water pail, only I put on two, one opposite to the other. After completing it I fastened it to a line five fathoms longer than the one I had and put it out, and it was a godsend indeed as it, coupled with the other, held us very nicely.

During the night, and especially the early hours of the morning, I was kept busy hauling in on the drogue line when I saw a very large sea coming and ease it off when it passed, which was tedious work. This was the morning of the 24th. Early in the forenoon we sighted a sail heading toward the westward and we were expecting she would get by without seeing us, but when she was within about a mile of us she veered from her course and ran down towards us. She proved to be an ocean steamship Batavia, from Liverpool for Boston, under command of Captain John E. Moreland.

As she came close to us the captain hailed us and asked if we wanted any assistance, to which I replied "No." He asked where we were bound, when I replied "to England." He then said that when he sighted us he thought it was a boat with survivors from some wrecked vessel. I then stood on deck holding on to my mainmast. He then asked if we wanted to be taken off, to which I again replied "No," but I said I should like to be reported. All this time handkerchiefs were waving from nearly every deadlight on the steamer. The captain gave us the lat. 44, lon. 48.20. We then parted company as the steamer proceeded on her course, dipping her flags as a salute to us to which we responded by dipping ours. The accompanying picture shows us as sketched by the mate of the steamer at the time, who presented it to me about six months after in New York, as I took dinner with him on board. The captain at the time gave me a letter certifying the fact of his speaking us at the time. Following is a copy of the letter :—

NEW YORK, Jan. 29th, 1878.

I hereby certify that I spoke the boat "New Bedford" in latitude 44.00 n., longitude 48.00 w., bound to England, and manned by a man and woman, at 9 A. M., June 20th,

BOAT IN GALE OF WIND WHEN STEAMSHIP "BATAVIA" SPOKE US.

1877. At that time they reported themselves in good condition and required nothing.

JOHN E. MORELAND,

Commander Cunard Steamship " Batavia."

As I had requested Captain Moreland to report us on his
arrival, the following which appeared in the daily papers
proved that he did so. The report read thus :—

CRAPO SPOKEN.

SEEN IN MID-OCEAN—ALL WELL—IN WANT OF NOTHING.

Cunard steamship Batavia arrived Monday at Boston,
from Liverpool, and reported that on Wednesday, June
20th, at 9.15 A. M., a small sailboat was sighted. The
steamer, after bearing down upon her, stopped within hailing distance. It proved to be the little boat New Bedford,
with Captain Thomas Crapo and wife on board. They
reported having experienced heavy weather, but were both
well and in want of nothing. The officers of the steamer
gave them their position as latitude 44 north, longitude 48
west.

The New Bedford, it will be remembered, sailed from
this port Monday, May 28th, and from Chatham, her real
point of departure, Saturday, June 2nd. She was last
spoken June 7th in lat. 42.20, lon. 64.22. She had sailed
in the neighborhood of 850 miles since previously spoken
and 1,140 miles since leaving Chatham.

I wish to state to my readers that there is a slight mis-
take in the report of the Batavia, as the paper stated that
she spoke us on the 20th of June, but it is entered in my
log book as the 24th, which was the time we were spoken.
I explain this so my readers will not be misled in the
dates and positions of our voyage.

The gale continued through the night with the ·seas

running mountains high with the wind from the westward. The boat labored very hard and the seas were continually breaking over her, which showed the velocity of the wind. About nine o'clock on the morning of the 25th I hauled in the drogue, which I had tended for the past eighteen hours, and proceeded on our course, steering east-southeast by the compass. We continued on through the day and the following night until daylight of the 26th, when I hove to and took a nap. When I awoke the sky was still very heavy and overcast, and no signs of the sun breaking through. The wind had moderated but the seas were still running very high; nothing but gulls and porpoises in sight, the porpoises many times coming so close to our boat that I could touch them. Later in the day the wind increased and again blew quite heavy, but we continued to run under our foresail.

Along towards night we sighted a Swansea brig, which ran down and spoke us. The captain says, "Give us a line and we will tow you." "We are not crossing the ocean that way," I replied. The seas were running so high and her name was so badly painted we could not make it out, all we could make out was the word Swansea. About an hour after speaking the brig we saw a very large sunfish, which measured, I should judge, all of three feet across the back. These sunfish are a very queer-looking fish, the under part very much resembling a scallop. They are not good for eating purposes; the only part I ever heard of being put to use was the liver which is very much sought for, as the oil from it is claimed to be very good for the relief of that painful disease, rheumatism.

We continued on through the night with a strong wind until about four o'clock in the morning of June 27th, when I took my usual nap, and after breakfast started again with the wind blowing from the southwest. I steered east by the compass to keep out of the trough of the sea as they were still running very high. And before noon it began to rain very hard, which soon wet me to the skin, and we began to ship large quantities of water, which made it very unpleasant for us. We ran along until about six o'clock in the afternoon when, owing to the increase of the wind and heavy seas, I again hove to and put out my drogue.

During the early hours of the night the wind took a slant to the northwest and increased in its fury but moderated again towards morning, so much so that about seven o'clock of the 28th I hauled in our drogue and proceeded on our course with the wind from the west. About nine o'clock in the forenoon we sighted a sail heading to the westward, and we were probably seen by them about the same time. We sighted them as they changed their course and headed for us, and as she arrived within hailing distance the captain hailed us. She proved to be the Bremen barque Amphitrite, from Bristol, England, bound to Quebec, under command of Captain Geares. He invited us to come on board, but we respectfully declined; but as the captain's wife urged us so hard we at last consented to go on board for a short time.

The captain then ordered the sailors to get down in our boat to fend her off and keep her from pounding against the side of the ship, and we then went on board. And what a relief that was to our tired and cramped limbs; simple words cannot adequately describe the sensation, as we had been cramped into a small compass where we could scarcely turn around for twenty-six days, and to once more be permitted to walk, run or jump was pleasure indeed. As we stepped on board we were greeted with applause from all on board, and the captain and his wife, who were a newly married couple, escorted us down into their cabin. At the same time issuing orders to haul aback the vessel's yards to keep her from sailing along.

We were pleasantly entertained while on board, and dinner was served and we all sat down, which also was very pleasing for us to have a chance to sit down and quietly partake of a well-prepared meal placed on a table and comfortable chairs to sit in.

We remained on board about three quarters of an hour. While on board I wrote two letters directed to New Bedford, which the captain was to mail for me upon his arrival in port. We then made preparations to go aboard of our boat again, and we were prevailed upon to accept two bottles of choice wine which we were very grateful for. We then went aboard and our lines were cast off, good-byes were said, and amid cheers from all we parted company and sailed on our course. The crew were waving handkerchiefs and hats as long as we could see them, to which we responded by dipping our colors.

During our conversation at dinner I requested the captain to report us upon his arrival, and to prove that he did the following shows, which was printed in the papers :

THE NEW BEDFORD REPORTED.

CAPTAIN AND MRS. CRAPO EAT DINNER ON BOARD
BARQUE AMPHITRITE.—THE VOYAGERS WELL.

Captain Geares of the barque Amphitrite, from Bristol, England, reported that June 26th, in lat. 44.39 north, lon. 43 west, met the twenty-foot boat (schooner rigged whaleboat) New Bedford, twenty-two days out, with Mr. and Mrs. Crapo on board. Hove to and the two voyagers boarded the Amphitrite. They remained to dinner and expressed themselves well satisfied so far with the voyage to Europe, and stated that they had enjoyed good health. At parting Captain Geares provided them with wine and

water and a few small articles, when the two vessels sepa-
rated, the New Bedford steering east-northeast, and the
ship's company gave them three cheers and wished them
Godspeed.

I wish here to call the attention of my readers to the fact
that the above report claims that the vessel spoke us June
26th, when in reality, according to my log, it was June
28th. Yet it does not matter which it is, only I don't wish
to make any false statements if possible.

We watched her until she disappeared from view, and
we were again alone upon the broad Atlantic with nothing
but water in sight. While on board the Amphitrite I
noticed that according to her compass mine was about two
points out, no doubt caused by my stepping on it. This
being so would be liable to carry us considerably farther to
the southward than we wanted to go, but I was now on
my guard and could steer accordingly. Later in the day
the wind took a slant, and began to blow quite heavy and
the seas began to make very rapidly, and to cap the climax
rain squalls set in which wet me to the skin. As the wind
increased I hove to and put out my drogue and laid to until
about five o'clock in the morning of the 29th, when we
hauled it in and proceeded on.

About ten in the forenoon we spoke the English barque
Pool Scar of Liverpool, from Lubec to the English Channel. After parting company with her the wind again increased and we outsailed the Pool Scar by leading her
about two miles. Later the wind canted to the northwest,
which gave her a chance to show us her heels as all of her
sails would now draw to a good advantage; she easily drew
along and passed us in the night. The captain gave us
the lon. as 37.12 by the chronometer. The morning of
the 30th dawned clear and beautiful, but the wind soon
began to blow quite heavily. The seas made fast and

the wind continued to increase so that the little boat labored
very heavily, and the seas were continually breaking over
her and I at last deemed it advisable to heave to. Our
bedding was completely saturated and everything very wet.
And to make it more uncomfortable, about four in the
afternoon a very heavy rainstorm set in and continued
through the night.

The wind began to moderate about 3 A. M. of July 1st,
and about five we hauled in our drogue and proceeded on
our course ; at about eleven the wind canted to the north
and light breezes prevailed with occasional rain squalls,
and about three in the afternoon it was a settled calm.
About five o'clock the wind backed into the northeast,
accompanied by heavy rain, which continued through the
night. Daylight of July 2d found us surrounded by heavy
storm clouds and the rain falling in torrents, and whales
appeared all around us. About nine o'clock I lay down
to sleep and told my wife to keep awake and keep a sharp
lookout. And I will here state just as she explains it.
Her story is this :

"I kept awake all night until about eleven o'clock, when
my eyes grew so heavy that I put fresh water on them to
try to keep them open ; I then put on salt water, as the
fresh did not appear to do any good, and this made them
awful sticky, but as they continued to draw together I lay
down and was asleep in a moment. Somewhat about one
o'clock I awoke with a start ; something seemed to be pulling me, and I jumped up at once and looking out saw a
large steamer heading directly for us. I halloed to my
husband to wake up at once, which he did and grabbed
our lantern, which was burning, and waved it aloft. The
steamer, as was lucky for us both, had a competent person
on lookout, as the minute he waved our lantern we could
see the steamer sheer to one side. We hailed but could

not understand their language; we supposed she was a German, but do not know.''

My readers can readily picture to themselves what our danger was, lying to without any breeze right in the track of passing vessels and both of us asleep. And it was fortunate for us that she awoke as she did, as it would only have been but a few seconds before she would have struck us, and no one aboard the large steamer would have been any the wiser. But thank heaven we were permitted to proceed without accident, but I made up my mind to do no more sleeping nights. About four in the morning a light breeze sprang up from the southward when we proceeded, steering east-southeast by the compass. About five o'clock rain squalls set in, and about ten in the forenoon we sighted the English barque Ontario of Windsor, Nova Scotia, from Hamburg for New York. We ran alongside and got a keg of fresh water as ours had become unfit for use, and we talked with them and they seemed to be pleased to see us. After we had put the keg of water they gave us into our water keg we thanked them and bade them good-bye.

About four in the afternoon a thick fog settled around which hung on through the early part of the night. After midnight it cleared and the wind breezed up from the southward, and about four o'clock in the morning I took a nap. This was on the third of July. When I awoke we again made sail and proceeded, and about the middle of the day a heavy thunderstorm set in, which was so heavy that we hove to and waited for it to pass over, but it was early in the morning of the fourth that the clouds dispersed and the stars peeped forth. This July 4th was lacking of the noise and rattle of a 4th on shore, and our minds were carried back to the little city of New Bedford as a reminder of the fact. The day opened quite clear and a moderate breeze, and later in the day we were left becalmed, but towards night it breezed up again and we sailed along on our course. July 5th opened with a clear sky and a moderate breeze from the southeast with nothing but water in sight. Early in the afternoon a heavy fog settled around us and held on until after midnight, and we had to sail by the wind as near our course as possible. Thus the day of July 6th passed.

About one in the morning of July 7th the fog had entirely disappeared and a moderate breeze was blowing from the southeast and we barely moved along. About six in the morning we sighted a sail which gradually drew nearer, and about 10 o'clock she was within hailing distance, when she spoke us. She proved to be the Norwegian barque Honor, bound for Cork. The captain gave us the longitude as 29.30. He, like all others, urged us to . come on board, but we respectfully declined. The captain also offered to provide us with anything they had on board, but we were not in want of anything, so amid cheers from the crew, we drifted apart and were soon out of sight of each other.

About two o'clock in the afternoon the wind freshened from the south and the sea made very fast. The sky was clear, but we had to work against a head sea which grew worse all the time. We could only make an east course by the compass, which was all of two points from our course. Thus we continued on, and about one in the early morning of the 8th the weather settled very cloudy, but the wind still held to the southward and the sea still held its own. During the forenoon the sea began to moderate. About ten o'clock of the same morning we sighted a steamer coming astern of us and approaching very fast. As she drew near she ran close and spoke us. She proved to be the ocean steamer Denmark, from New York to London, England. The engines were stopped and we were asked to come on board, which we did not see fit to do, but I ran towards her and as we drew near a line was thrown to us which I caught and made fast around our foremast and we were drawn alongside. Two of the crew were then ordered down to pass us provisions, which it seemed were all prepared for us unsolicited. They also presented us with a keg of water which I lashed to my mainmast for the time being. The captain and crew were very good to us and seemed to think they could not do enough for us. We thanked them all for the favors shown us, and with well wishes for our safe arrival we cast off and proceeded, amid cheers from all on board. The captain also gave us the correct longitude as 27.26, and the steamer's engines were again put in motion and thus we parted, and she soon disappeared from view. On arriving in England Capt. Williams gave me the following letter :

S. S. DENMARK,
LONDON, December, 1877.

CAPT. CRAPO,

Dear Sir: As you are now about leaving England, and some people have been sceptical as to your crossing the Atlantic in the small boat ''New Bedford,'' you are at perfect liberty to use my testimony as to passing you at sea on your voyage, viz : July 7th, 7.30 p. m., latitude 47.12 n. ; 27° 33 west.

ROBERT P. WILLIAMS,
Master National Steamship Co.'s S. S. Denmark,
of Liverpool.

About two in the afternoon the wind freshened and we experienced very heavy squalls. During the afternoon, about four o'clock, I furled my foresail and took a short nap. About 8.30 I woke and proceeded, with the weather very thick ; our course by compass was southeast by east half east. Thus we continued on, and the 9th opened with the wind from the same quarter and a heavy rainstorm set in ; this coupled with a heavy cross sea made it very uncomfortable for us. My readers can readily imagine what a drenching rainstorm at sea, in a small boat, must be, as a heavy storm on shore can easily be taken as an illustration. Yet we had to take it, and no matter how wet we were we had no means of drying our clothes only in the open air, aided by the sun, which did not shine every day as my readers can see.

About ten o'clock I furled the mainsail and ran under our foresail until about midnight. The sea continued to make and occasionally broke over the boat, so at last I decided to lay to. I furled the foresail and set the mainsail for a storm trysail and put out my drogue; thus the morning of the 10th found us. Thus we lay until daylight when the seas began to moderate, so we again started on our course, steering east-southeast by the compass. Later in the day we sighted two barques on the wind heading to the southward. They came within about two miles of us, but as they were beating on the wind they probably did not deem it advisable to bother about us, so we soon were out of sight of each other.

About two in the afternoon the sky settled darker than before and the wind continued to blow very heavily. About nine o'clock in the evening we sighted a vessel's red light, which is carried on the port side. We ran within about a quarter of a mile of her, and as she proceeded her light soon disappeared from view. About 11 o'clock the wind changed to west-southwest and light rains continued to follow us, and the morning of the eleventh found the weather about the same. At daylight I took a short nap. When I awoke we again started, with a moderate breeze and a heavy sky and sea, steering east-southeast by the

compass; light baffling winds prevailed. I now found time
to put the water given to us by the captain of the Denmark
into our water kegs, so after doing so I threw the keg overboard. After doing so I glanced around and saw a vessel
in the distance, and as she was not a great distance off I
headed for her, expecting of course that we were seen by
those on board. As I neared her I hailed her, when a dog
on board began to bark. I hailed several times, and at
last made myself heard, when all hands came to the side of
the vessel and appeared thunderstruck to see us in such a
small boat. At last the captain found his voice and
hailed, when I asked what the longitude was. He asked
us to come alongside, but I told him we could not as we
were in a hurry, so we sailed on, and as we drew apart he
shouted the longitude, 25, so I thanked him, and the crew
cheered lustily.

Light baffling winds continued until about three in the
morning of the 12th, when I again took a nap. Started
again about eight o'clock, with a light breeze from the
northwest. We sailed along very pleasantly until about
eight in the evening, when the wind canted to the westward and it soon settled very cloudy, which made the sky
as black as ink.' Then rain began to fall in torrents and
the wind howled. About two in the morning of the 13th
I hove to and put out my drogue, and had a short sleep.
While I was asleep the weather cleared, so about nine in
forenoon we again started, steering east by south half-
south by the compass. About ten the wind began to increase and the seas began to make very fast. We sighted
a bark steering to the eastward, which passed within a
half a mile of us. About one in the morning of the 14th
heavy squalls set in, and about three I hove to for a nap,
and started again about nine in a heavy rainstorm. About
four in the afternoon we sighted two vessels, steering to the

southward, the rain still falling in torrents, and about one in the morning of the 15th I decided to heave to and put out my drogue, which I did. My wife had begun to feel quite bad. I suppose the change from canned goods to fresh meat and vegetables given to us from the Denmark was the cause. This made it very uncomfortable for both of us, as we were not provided with a supply of medicines, and a doctor was out of the question. Sickness is not pleasant at any time, even when a doctor lives next door to you, and to be where one cannot be had for love or money was decidedly bad.

We both thought it would soon pass off, but it did not seem to do so, as she complained of feeling worse as the time passed on. I was dead tired, so I took a short nap, after which we again proceeded. The wind canted to the north-northwest, and the weather cleared. About eleven the wind increased and the sea made very fast, and as it grew worse all the time I deemed it advisable to heave to, as our little boat labored very heavy. The seas were terrible and I had grave fears for our safety, as the seas were continually breaking over her. The morning of the 16th found us in the same predicament, and no signs of the gale abating. About seven o'clock in the morning, the Bremen barque Astronom spoke us and asked if we wanted any assistance, or if we wanted to come on board, as we appeared to be in a sad condition; but we had stood it thus far, and I thought we could stand it a little longer. Yet I could but help thinking of my wife, who grew decidedly worse each day. A terrible weakness had taken hold of her, and she often said she did not care whether she ever reached England or not. Yet in the face of all this we declined to accept any assistance, and thanked them very courteously for their proffered help; so we parted and were soon out of sight of each other, as it did not take her long in the strong wind, as she was scudding before it, while we had to lay to.

Shortly after she left us our rudder head was twisted off, which was a bad go for us, but luckily I had a spare one and could replace it as soon as the weather would permit, but at the present time the boat was rolling and pitching about like an eggshell. About five o'clock in the afternoon a Prussian brig passed close to us, heading to the eastward, and was soon lost to view. Thus we rocked and rolled through the day and night, and about six o'clock in the morning of the 17th we sighted a barque under short sail heading to the eastward. There was no apparent change in the weather until about five o'clock in the morning of the 18th, when the wind canted to north-northwest and moderated. As the signs held good about six o'clock the same morning I got out my spare rudder and rigged it and made sail and started again, steering east by north by the compass. The seas were still running very high and the waves dashed across the boat at every jump. The sky cleared, which made it a little more inviting for us; yet it was not much pleasure at best. Mrs. Crapo was still very much under the weather, and was unable to render any assistance whatever.

About four o'clock in the afternoon the wind changed to west-southwest, and fog and rain again set in. I don't remember in all of my going to sea and crossing the Atlantic ocean so many times, of seeing a period of time that we had been on our passage with so many gales and so much fog and rain; and I have thought a great many times since that if I had taken a more northerly course I probably would have had a better passage. The Atlantic ocean is a very rough place during the winter months, but is generally quite good during the summer. Yet we were having nearly as rough a passage as if it were winter instead of in the summer.

Words cannot express, even to sailors themselves, what we experienced on that passage. Gales that were terrible to encounter, especially in a little boat, when many large vessels have been wrecked in gales of less magnitude. Yet there we were, day and night, and I slept on an average of four hours out of each twenty-four during the passage, and not a ghost of a chance to move about enough to keep one's blood in circulation. At all times, especially in heavy weather, my thoughts would turn to my wife who was bearing up bravely under the ordeal, especially as sick as she was, and as she grew worse instead of better plagued me more, I think, than it did her. Of course all I could do under the circumstances was to cheer her up all I possibly could.

If she had had a good, dry, comfortable bed to lie on it would have been far better, but our readers can see how limited our accommodations were. It was bad enough for her to be obliged to put up with it when she was feeling well and happy, but now the thought was as wormwood, and I must make all possible haste to reach land where medical aid could be had for her, as she was growing very despondent and made the remark a great many times that she did not believe she would live to see or reach land again, and also that she did not care whether she did or not. But the Lord was merciful to us all through, and we put our trust in Him and sailed on.

About two o'clock in the morning of the 19th I again hove the boat to as the weather was so bad I deemed it unsafe to run, as I did not wish to venture any chances. I watched very closely for signs of its moderating and at last was rewarded by signs of a change of wind, when we again started, although it was not pleasant sailing. But we were all the time drawing nearer to our destination, which meant a great deal to us.

Very soon a thick fog set in and rain began to fall very heavily, which continued until about half past six o'clock in the evening, when the fog lifted a little. As the fog lifted we sighted a barque which proved, as we drew up to her, to be an English barque from Baltimore to Hamburg. The captain gave us the latitude as 48.20, lon. 11.50. Cheers from the crew rent the air, to which we heartily responded; we continued on our way, and again the weather began to moderate. About three o'clock in the morning of the 20th it again settled foggy, and remained so until about 10 o'clock, when it lifted and the sun soon broke through, with the wind from the westward and blowing quite heavily.

Several vessels were in sight and we ran close to one, a brig named Susan, and the captain gave us the lat. 49.32, lon. 7.30, also the distance as fifty-five miles from Scilly. He wanted us to run alongside, but the wind blew so hard and the seas ran so high I did not dare to attempt it, but continued on towards our destination, first thanking the captain for the desired information. This was very encouraging to us. We were nearing our long-looked-for destination, and with good luck we would soon enter a safe anchorage, and my wife could then have medical attention.

When daylight of the 21st appeared it was very foggy, which held on until about ten o'clock, when it lifted. As it lifted we sighted a steamer. We ran towards her, and as we drew near I asked the captain how Scilly Island bore and he answered by pointing for me, and as I looked I could see the land. Oh! what a welcome sight. Words cannot adequately express the delight we felt upon seeing it before our eyes and we lost no time in heading for it, but owing to a strong current and wind we were about five miles to the leeward when we got abreast of them, so

I kept off for Land's End, and as we passed the lighthouse about four o'clock in the afternoon the keeper dipped his colors to us and rang his bell. We continued on, saluting him in return as we passed. We arrived in Newland, Penzance, at eleven o'clock in the night and ran alongside of a fishing boat which I hailed, but got no reply, as there was no one on board, so I made my boat fast and told Mrs. Crapo we would have some good hot coffee.

So, although it was late and I was tired, having steered the boat without any rest for the past seventy-two hours, I felt so encouraged to think our perilous voyage was over I lit our oil stove and put on our little giant coffeepot. We both sat down watching it, and both fell fast asleep as we sat there and did not wake up until daylight had broke. My left hand was useless from steering so long and steadily, and I was as bad off as if I did not have any at all, but of course I expected it would regain itself in a short time.

· Our long, perilous voyage was over, and here we were, on a Sunday morning, made fast to a fishing boat belonging to some inhabitant of the British Isles. We then filled our lamp stove again, as it had burned itself out while we were sitting around it asleep, and made ourselves a good cup of coffee, which seemed to taste far better to us than it had at any time during our voyage. Mrs. Crapo's condition was such as to make anything, no matter how palatable, have a queer flat taste, and we were both very anxious to get ashore where medical aid could be had to assist her in regaining her former health. As she clothed herself entirely in flannel during the voyage we did not expect any serious results would follow, yet when she got wet during heavy weather or rainstorms, a change had to be made as soon as convenient, and many times the change would be very damp, especially when heavy weather held on for any length of time.

As we had no means of drying any clothes, excepting in the sun, and as my readers already know there were a great many times when the sun did not shine for several days, not only our clothes would be wet, but our bedding besides, and everyone knows that a damp bed is not a pleasant place to seek for a quiet undisturbed rest. Many times the bed was so wet that when placed in the sun it would steam for a long time, and as I had nothing of any account to do while steering I would watch the fine vapor arise until it was again perfectly dry. After drinking our coffee I managed to climb up my foremast and rove my signal halliards to hoist my colors with.

I found it a very difficult task as my hand was as I have stated, entirely useless, and might as well have been cut off for all the good it was at present. My colors had not been set long before we saw a boat approaching, which soon came alongside. The man who was its only occupant asked us a great many questions and seemed to be much pleased to be the one to welcome us upon our safe arrival. He also asked if we wished to go on shore, and as that was our earnest desire he volunteered to land us at once. As we neared the shore we saw a lady coming down towards the place where we would land. This gave Mrs. Crapo fresh courage, to see one of her sex ready to welcome her, and as we stepped on shore she invited us to go to her house, which was close by, and have some hot tea.

We accepted this kind invitation and went to her house, when a steaming cup of hot tea and a tempting breakfast was placed before us. As we had been drinking coffee during our voyage tea was quite acceptable, and we again enjoyed a good hearty meal sitting at a well-regulated table whose comforts were far different from what we had to put up with for the past forty-nine days, and I was much pleased to see Mrs. Crapo—by the way, she had eaten very sparingly since the first attack of sickness—eating quite a breakfast and seemingly enjoying it very much.

It was surprising to see how the news of our arrival spread. The crowds gathered about the house waiting for a chance to see us. Hundreds entered and shook hands with us and appeared perfectly satisfied if they could only do so, or if they could only touch us in any way they were satisfied. Mrs. Crapo was the lion of the hour. A woman to cross the tempestuous Atlantic ocean in a small boat like ours was what turned the people's heads, and all seemed to be pleased to receive a word from her. Even to our dishes and utensils used during our memorable voyage were eagerly sought for as mementoes, and as some were silver-plated the recipients had the dates of our sailing and arriving neatly engraved upon them. During the day religious services were held in the little church especially for us, which were attended by a large number of people.

Every kindness was shown us by the Cornish people, and we were graciously received by all. We remained at the house of the lady during our stay, and it was stated to us that more people visited us and turned out to see us than did on the arrival of the Prince and Princess of Wales a short time before. Mrs. Crapo had now nearly regained her former health, thanks to the skill of a physician recommended to us by our landlady, whose medicines worked a great change from the start. Every day we were there hundreds came to see us; many came from a long distance on purpose to do so.

On the 27th of the same month we bade them good-bye, and with thanks to our hostess for her kind attention during our stay under her roof, we left for Penzance. We again entered our frail craft and started. The distance was only three miles, and with a fair breeze it did not take us long to go. On our arrival hundreds had gathered to see us,

attracted by our flags while sailing along, and as the crowd
increased in numbers I did as I was asked by many of
them, which was to sail around a little while so the crowd
could view the boat and watch her sailing qualities. I
sailed around for them nearly an hour, and I thought the
crowd would go wild when we ran alongside of the wharf.

After making fast I proceeded to take the masts out of
her. After doing so I then took out my five water kegs,
—we had only used from one which held twenty gallons,
as this one was replenished by passing vessels at different
times. I let what remained run overboard and then
knocked out the bungs from the others to do the same.
Owing to the kegs being bunged up tight caused the water
to be bad and unfit for use, providing we had exhausted our
other supply, and as I turned them over to let it run out it
was as thick as jelly and was not fit for anything. Thus
eighty gallons of the one hundred put in the boat at New
Bedford before starting was thrown overboard at Penzance.
If I had left the bungs loose when stowing them in the
boat would probably saved it all, but be that as it may we
were not without during the voyage and a fresh supply was
tendered by every vessel we spoke.

After emptying the kegs I put slings on the boat and
hoisted her out with a crane on the wharf. As she hung
in mid-air a gentleman approached and asked me if I was
willing he took a photograph of her as she hung, to which
I willingly consented, and he made preparations to do so.
A large multitude of people were present at the time. After
he had taken the photographs I had her put on board of
the cars and we started for London, where we arrived the
next morning.

We were met at the depot by my wife's father, who had
been on the lookout for us for several days, so we accompanied him to his home. During the forenoon he and I

THE "NEW BEDFORD" BEING HOISTED OUT OF WATER AT PENZANCE, ENGLAND.

paid a visit to the American Consul when I delivered up
my papers, or rather the letter given to me by the Custom
House officials at New Bedford, as was explained in the
first part of the voyage. And below is a copy of his given
to me:

United States Consulate General, London.
Exhibited at this Office, July 28th, 1877.
J. VINING,
Vice Consul General and Shipping
Commissioner at London.

No wonder he looked at me when he read the letter, as
such a marine document had never passed through his
hands before, and to enter such records of so small a craft
was novel in itself. He asked a great many questions
about our trip across and said he was more than pleased to
welcome us. We remained and talked for quite a length
of time, and then started back to my wife's father's home.
On our arrival we found that there had been three or four
agents of museums and shows to try to make arrangements
with us to exhibit ourselves and boat. One was an agent
for an aquarium, and one from the Alexander Palace.
The others did not say what they represented.

Early in the afternoon we went to the Alexander Palace,
and it did not take long to complete arrangements.

This Alexander Palace, as it is called, is a grand affair.
The large brick building covers a great many acres, to all
appearances, and the grounds cover a great many more.
The show consists of circus, minstrel, museum, opera,
drama, aquarium, horse racing, cricket, base ball, and a
hundred and one other things too numerous to mention.
We were engaged at a large salary, and the crowds that
flocked around us was surprising. There was no end to
the questions asked, which must at all times be answered

civilly. Many times the same question would be asked
dozens of times during the day and evening, which, though
very aggravating, must be put up with, as we were hired
to answer questions and must treat every one with due
respect.

Several of the Royal Family attended while we were
there. The out-door exhibitions in the evening were magnificent, to say the least, and crowds were going and coming all the time. The price of admission only entitled the
holder of the ticket to an entrance to the building, then
each performance had a cash price of its own. To take in
the whole affair would take several days and nights, and
would cost quite a little sum of money besides. There is
nothing in the United States that can begin to compare with
it. We remained there about six weeks and were visited
by thousands of people, each one elbowing their way to
get as near to us as possible, and the rush held on from
early morn until late at night. As fast as one would draw
out others took their places.

After completing our contract, we contracted to go to
. Liverpool to a place called Rockferry Garden, on the
Berkenhead side. We had no trouble in securing large
salaries, as the head ones knew that the crowds attracted to
see us would be large, and so they were. Sea captains,
young and old, visited us, and many wondered how I came
to take such a dangerous voyage, knowing the ocean as I
did; one in particular, an old gray-haired veteran, came
several times to see and talk with us about the passage.

Sea-faring men in particular forced their way in where
they could shake hands with us, and Mrs. Crapo was surrounded most of the time by the gentler sex, who seemed
to admire her courage in risking her life in such a frail
craft. The same questions were asked over and over again.
Everybody seemed to want to ask something; our auto-

graphs were asked for by hundreds of people, and we did our best to please everybody. We remained there about five weeks, when we started for Oldham to fill an engagement there. We exhibited in what is called the Alexander skating rink. We remained two weeks, when we went to Brighton, a well-known watering place. We exhibited at the King's Road skating rink, where we were again surrounded by large crowds of people. We remained there for a long time.

We were visited a great many times by a gentleman named Ashbury, or Ashbrey, who, at the time, was awaiting the arrival of President Grant in his tour around the world. He told us that he would do his best to have the President call on us during his stay. On his arrival at the gentleman's home we sent a written invitation to him, but as his time was about all taken up he could not do so, but after his departure we received a letter from Mr. Ashbury's Secretary stating that the President sent us his regrets in not being able to call on us, as he would have been pleased to do so. The letter was burned in the car at the fire at Mobley, Mo.

After completing our engagement we went to a place called Worthing, about twelve miles from Brighton, where we exhibited in another rink. We remained about two weeks, and during the time were visited by thousands who came expressly to see us. From there we returned to Brighton again and exhibited in what is called the Brighton west pier, which is a promenade built out over the water. We remained there about two weeks when we again returned to London, where we secured passage on the ocean steamship Canada. Our boat was brought over free of charge, and a pleasant time we had. We left London for New York Jan. 4th, 1878, and was sixteen days on the passage, which was far pleasanter than our passage over.

Everything was done that we could wish for to make it pleasant for us.

Mrs. Crapo especially enjoyed the return passage very much. On our arrival in New York we were much sought for by agents of museums and other shows. My wife strongly objected to exhibiting in a museum, no matter what the salary was that was offered. We therefore hired a place on Broadway and exhibited the boat about two weeks. At that time there was a large company at Gilmore's Garden, now called Madison Square Garden. We closed the place on Broadway and went there. While there we engaged to join a circus that at that time was in winter quarters, but was soon to open at the Garden. When they opened we were assigned a place in the menagerie where the crowds flocked around us, asking all sorts of questions; the American people take the cake in asking questions, and they kept us quite busy. We sold hundreds of photographs of ourselves and boat. We remained there about six weeks, when we started on the road. When exhibiting our boat we had her two masts in and all sail set and she could be seen from one end of the tent to the other, so everybody flocked around us to get a close view of her.

Right here I wish to say that the news of our sail across the Atlantic and our safe arrival was daily commented on and many papers and magazines inserted long pieces about it. The London Standard of July 23rd, just after our arrival, printed a long and accurate account which was copied by many others. The New York Police News copied it, and through its medium it was well circulated. The book called the Young Scientist gave a good and lengthy description of our voyage, coupled with pictures of situations. We have in our possession many papers which spoke very nicely about it, also many that are

printed in other languages which we do not understand,
yet we keep them as mementoes of our eventful voyage.
I here call my reader's attention to one from a correspon-
dent dated Penzance, Sunday (which was the day we
went on shore on our arrival in England), which will give
a' fair idea of the others.   It read thus:
   '' I was startled this morning, just at the commencement
of church, to hear that the boat which had left America
for England, with only a man and woman on board, had
arrived at Penzance.   On glancing along the promenade
I saw right away under Newlyn, a little boat with two
masts lying at anchor, whilst surrounding her were a clus-
ter of Newlyn boats filled with spectators who had come
to see the wonderful little craft.   The New Bedford is a
boat about twenty feet long, and of the registered tonnage
of one and sixty-two one hundredths, a little over one and
one-half tons.   ˙
   '' She carries two masts, one anchor and a drogue.   She
is built of cedar and is rigged as what is known as ' leg of
mutton rigged schooner.'   The name of the owner is Captain Thomas Crapo, aged thirty-five, who with his wife has
so bravely crossed the Atlantic in so tiny a craft.   The
voyage was commenced on May 28th, when the little vessel
left New Bedford, but by stress of weather she had to put
into Chatham, Massachusetts, where she stayed until the
second of June, when the sails were again hoisted, and the
little pigmy left on her perilous voyage with a fair wind.''
   It then goes on to illustrate what we passed through,
which my readers are already familiar with, and ends up
thus:
   '' Among the many extraordinary things connected with
the voyage is that it had to be run by dead reckoning, as
the New Bedford was not large enough to carry a chronometer.   Captain and Mrs. Crapo seemed wonderfully well

after the hardships they had undergone, though the captain
has a bad hand, and when he came ashore it was firmly
clenched through being forced to steer for seventy hours
without rest.

" The house they stopped at was invaded by a multitude
of people eager to shake hands with so brave a couple.
The boat was also an object of interest and was admired
by hundreds of people.

" No one knows the loneliness of the ocean but those who
have experienced it, and apart from the question of peril,
which probably the captain would not dwell upon too
strongly, the pair must have known that they were undertaking a task as trying to the brain from its monotony as to
the physical powers from its constant strain upon them.

" Luckily the only accident was a broken rudder and the
loss of a trifling item of gearing, and the lady's greatest
complaint is that she could not sleep for the whales, and
the captain's was that he could not stretch his limbs. His
hand is still numb from his hard labor at the tiller, but will
undoubtedly be all right again in a short time."

At last we were booked for the season to travel with
Howe's great London circus, and left New York for Nor-
walk, Conn., Sunday, May 28th, where we were to exhibit
the following day. We exhibited in most of the large
cities throughout New Hampshire, Massachusetts, Rhode
Island, Connecticut, New York, Pennsylvania, Ohio, Indi-
ana, Illinois, Missouri, Kansas, Iowa, Tennessee, Wiscon-
sin, and West Virginia. The most exciting experience
while with them was while we were asleep in the train,
which was sidetracked at Moberly, Missouri, when all of a
sudden some one cried fire, and on looking out of the win-
dow we saw that the baggage car which contained the baggage of the show, including many of our clothes and
presents given to us in England, was a mass of flames.

Everything was burned to ashes before our eyes, as there was no chance whatever to put the fire out. Nothing was left but the iron work, which was the only part that would not burn. We were very sorry to lose our things, especially our presents, but it could not be helped so we had to make the best of it. The last place we exhibited with them was in Brooklyn. As we had been roaming around with them about six months we decided to leave and return to New Bedford with our boat, which we did, and as we had done as we intended to in crossing to England, we were not ashamed to return to our starting place, as we had the laugh all on our side this time.

I remained in New Bedford through the winter, and in the spring I bought a schooner named the James Parker, Sr., of a hundred and five tons burthen, and started in the coasting trade as captain and owner. Mrs. Crapo went with me and had a good chance to see considerable of the country along the coast; we carried a great many different cargoes during the season, some up the Connecticut and Hudson rivers. Early in November I laid her alongside the wharf at New London, Conn., for the winter. Mrs. Crapo and myself kept house on board and took as much comfort as though installed in a mansion. We could go ashore when we chose and have just as good times.

Early in the following spring I had a good offer for the vessel, so I accepted it and returned to New Bedford, where I remained but a few days when I bought another one named the Adelia Felicia, of a 120 tons register. My first cargo was for Middletown, Conn., and as soon as I arrived I sent for Mrs. Crapo to join me, which she did. We sailed her throughout the summer until nearly Christmas, when I hauled alongside the wharf at New Bedford for the winter, and started again in the spring, running to and from different ports from Maine to Virginia, wherever we could get a paying cargo, and late in the fall we again put in at New Bedford for winter quarters.

The following spring we started again and took a cargo wherever or whenever we could get it. We continued through the warm months and as soon as cold weather set in we hauled up this time at Wareham, on Cape Cod, Massachusetts. When warm weather opened we again began plying our trade and continued to do so until Sept. 1883, when I sold the vessel. I sold her while lying at anchor at Port Chester, New York, and was to deliver her at Perth Amboy, New Jersey, as soon as we discharged our cargo. After delivering her, Mrs. Crapo and myself returned to New Bedford and settled down to housekeeping, as my wife declared she was not going to sea any more.

In March of the following year I bought the schooner Gustie Wilson, of a hundred and forty-one tons register, and ran her through the season. As cold weather set in I chartered to go to the West Indies. I went from the West Indies to Maracaibo to load for New York. On arriving at Maracaibo I had to take on a pilot and go up the lagoon about one hundred and fifty miles. The scenery was quite pleasing, and many houses could be seen built on spiles out into the water. And alligators, there was no end to them; the lagoons were full of them. The pilot and I took the schooner's boat and went up a small bay, or lagoon, as they are called, and had great sport shooting at them. I fired all the cartridges I had and would have fired many more if I had had them.

Their skins were so tough that a bullet from a revolver didn't seem to have much effect on them. Nevertheless we enjoyed it as much as though every shot we fired had killed one. They would drag themselves up on the bank and lay for hours with their eyes shut and you would think they were dead, but touch them in any way they would soon show you to the contrary. As we had no more cartridges to fire at them we went on board and continued on our way up the lagoon. Upon reaching our destination we anchored in about three fathoms of water, and we began to make preparations for receiving our cargo. We were to load cedar logs, which were rafted out to us by men on shore.

While loading, I went on deck one day after finishing my dinner, and on looking around I saw what appeared to be the smoke from a steamer. I spoke of it to the pilot who had not yet finished his dinner. I said, ''Here is a steamer coming our way.'' In a few minutes he came on deck, and on looking in the direction I pointed he smiled and says, '' That is no steamer,'' whereupon I inquired what it was if it wasn't a steamer. '' Well,'' says he, ''that is a flock of mosquitoes.'' I looked at him, thinking he was joking me, but I saw he was in earnest. I had heard of clouds of mosquitoes, but had never seen one before. They were actually so thick that they would darken the sun like a cloud passing before it.

I watched them for a considerable length of time, hoping they would draw nearer, but they seemed to remain about the same distance away as at first. What a sad predicament a fellow would be in surrounded by a cloud of hungry mosquitoes, especially in a swamp where he could not get any shelter from them. He would stand a poor show of getting out alive, as they would suck every particle of blood he had in him in a very short time. I found before I left there that it was no unusual sight to see large clouds of them, as they made their appearance several times during our stay.

We loaded all the logs they had and then went down to Maracaibo to take on enough to complete our cargo. As

SCHOONER GUSTIE WILSON LEAVING NEW YORK FOR JACKSONVILLE.

soon as we finished loading we sailed for New York, and experienced a very rough passage, but we arrived without serious accident and discharged our cargo and chartered to load coal at Elizabethport, New Jersey, for Province-town, on Cape Cod. From Provincetown I ran in at New Bedford and hauled up for several days, as there was so much ice in the bay it was not much pleasure to try to run, as freights were so low and it took so long to go from one place to the other there was not much left after paying expenses, so I thought I would wait a few days to see if some of the ice wouldn't drift out to sea.

While at the wharf I had a good offer for her, and I decided to let her remain my property a while longer at least. I chartered to take a cargo from Haverstraw to Mosquito Inlet, Florida; we loaded brick, cement and other material for masons use. We had 80,000 brick on board and had to land them through the surf, which was a dangerous task. All had to be carried in our yawl boat, and as we neared the shore we had to jump overboard and hold on to the boat to keep her from tipping over and spilling the brick; she was nearly half full of water every time we carried a load ashore, where the surf would dash over her. It was tedious work and took us about two weeks. We were wet through from daylight to dark, which was not very pleasant, yet as the water was warm we did not suffer much from exposure. It was a pleasing sound when it was announced that we had the last of them.

After unloading we sailed for Jacksonville, Florida, to load hard pine for New London, Connecticut. From there I went to New Bedford, where I remained about three weeks. During my stay a schooner arrived loaded with corn for parties in New Bedford. While entering the harbor she struck on a rock, and by the time she reached the wharf she sank. I was chartered to take the cargo out of her and load it into my vessel, which took us about a week, working a large gang day and night.

We finished at last and started for New York, where we arrived safe and sound and began unloading, which was a very hard job, as the corn was a dirty, soggy mess, and we were glad when it was all out. From there we sailed to Elizabethport and loaded coal for Wareham. After discharging we returned to New York and chartered to load for Jacksonville, Florida. Our cargo consisted of material for life-saving stations. At this time I agreed to take two more cargoes of the same kind down the Florida coast. We had more or less rough weather, but nothing serious happened.

The brick, paint, oils and cement we had to carry on shore in our yawl boat, and about every time we went ashore in her she would capsize in the surf, and we had to keep our eyes open and get it on shore before it got spoiled in the surf. The lumber and shingles we rafted ashore; the surf was so heavy that every time we rafted a load ashore the raft would go to pieces and scatter it all along the beach, and it was fortunate that there was a large gang on shore to catch it or a great deal would probably have been lost. We had this to go through in five different places where a certain quantity was to be left. After finishing the last, which was put ashore up the Injun River, we went to Jacksonville, where we were to load hard pine for New York.

While unloading I was chartered to take a load of hard pine from Jacksonville to St. Thomas in the West Indies, and was allowed the privilege of taking a cargo to Jacksonville, which would be far better for me than to go empty. I found a cargo at last and proceeded to put it on board. It consisted of 147 1-2 tons of railroad iron; not a very desirable cargo, but it was take that or nothing, and as I

was in a hurry I took it.   The worst of all was that we had
to keep about forty ton on deck.   All sailors object to a
deck load, and are none to blame for it, as it is always in
the way, especially in heavy weather or a gale of wind.
I had at the time a crew of six men, so with plenty of help
we were ready for a start in a very short time after we
began loading.

We left New York August 18th, and had very good
weather, and by the 25th we were off Cape Hatteras in
company with a fleet of about twenty other vessels, and
the wind was beginning to blow very strong from the
southwest, and before night set in the sky was very heavy
and the wind was howling through the rigging.   The
wind increased as the night went by, and before morning
it was blowing a hurricane; the swell had changed to a
heavy sea and the vessel's rails were under water most of
the time.   Our cargo was a dead weight in her.   If it had
been lumber or some buoyant material she would have
behaved far better.   These are the times when good seamanship is required to weather a gale, yet with a cargo of
iron we stood a very poor show.

But we would do all that could be done, and if there was
any chance of saving the vessel and cargo we would do so.
And rain, how it did pour down; we did not mind it very
much as we were all wet completely through already by the
seas breaking over the vessel.   For several hours we ran
with her prow pointing right into the gale.   We did not
dare to show much canvas for the gale was growing more
and more furious all the time, and she had all she could
do to live in such an angry sea.

At three o'clock Wednesday morning, Aug. 26th, a re-
markable incident occurred.   The wind suddenly ceased
and for about two minutes there was a dead calm.   The
waves raised by the gale were running fifty or sixty feet

high, and our little schooner was one moment on the crest of a tremendous billow and the next she would sink way down in the trough with her masts barely reaching above the crest of the high seas.

The lull in the storm was very brief and I was about to put more sail on her when the wind came from the north-east, which my readers will see was directly opposite from what it had been blowing and blew harder than ever. The wind was blowing at least seventy miles an hour. With the wind blowing in one direction and the seas running in another made the water fearfully rough, and it required good seamanship to keep her heading right. Had we been caught in such a way as to bring her side to the storm, with the wind against her on one side and the heavy seas on the other would have foundered her in a moment's time, but we were very fortunate so far in keeping her head into it.

About half past five we shipped a heavy sea which carried away our jib-boom and started a leak in our knight-heads, and it now began to look dark for us. She would in all probability make water very fast as she was straining so heavily. And to make matters worse our fore-topmast was carried away, which made her labor very hard. I soon discovered that she was taking in water faster than I had anticipated she would, and I made up my mind that unless the gale abated very speedily there was no hope for us, and by seven o'clock I told the crew to make ready to abandon her to her fate.

All we had to depend on now was our small boat, a yawl used for taking a line to shore or to go ashore in, or, in fact, she came in handy a great many times, especially at this time. Now the question of the moment was, could we launch her safely in such a furious sea? and the only answer to it was try and see, which we did, and joy of joys, we landed her right side up with care into that seething sea, and as she struck the water I jumped into her to hold her alongside, at the same time calling to my crew to get in as quick as possible as the boat was in imminent danger of being crushed against the side of the vessel, but, luckily, no such misfortune befell us.

Our cook, a colored man from Boston, tried to catch some lumber thrown overboard by the crew in case the boat tipped over, and it swept out of his reach as he either fell or jumped into the seething sea without catching hold of anything. All of us in the boat saw his head once as he came to the top of the water, but he was dead. The furious sea that had been so destructive to the schooner by tumbling her about caught the yawl boat as though it was a chip and tossed it high in the air and then let it drop into the hollow of the waves, and it looked as though it would be smashed to pieces any moment.

We had not left the schooner five minutes before she careened. One rail went down under water and the next minute she disappeared altogether, going down bow first. Such was her fate, and what ours would be the Lord only knew. I don't know whether anyone but ourselves saw her go down, but it was a sorry sight, especially for us, and left as we were, yet there were other vessels not a great distance off, battling with the wind and waves in order to remain afloat. We had not been in the boat a half hour when she was swamped by cross seas and she turned over as quick as a flash, but luckily we were on our guard and scrambled for the bottom of her, which was now the top.

I got a good hold and kept it, but the other four were not so fortunate as a large sea took them away, but the next one brought them back and they succeeded in getting back to and on top of the boat. Sometimes we were

WRECK OF THE SCHOONER GUSTIE WILSON.

thrown forty or fifty feet away from the boat but managed to get back again. After a while she righted and we again got inside, but very soon she was again sent whirling over and over and we were all struggling to get back. I should judge it was about eight o'clock when Daniel Cume, a seaman from Middletown, Connecticut, was swept off, and being very much exhausted he did not have the strength to get back, so he was lost. This left us only four out of our crew of six, and unless we were rescued very soon there would be none left to tell the story.

At last we saw a large two-masted schooner coming towards us and our courage arose at once, but those on board did not appear to see us as she swept on and was soon lost to view. The wind still howled and we began to look our fate squarely in the face ; such times as these a person thinks, if he ever does, and rapidly too. Every few minutes some of us would be washed off, and none of us could tell who would be the next victim claimed by mother ocean. I knew there must be other vessels close by, but the sea was so rough we could not be seen a half of a mile.

I honestly believe I was swept off the boat at least a hundred times but was always fortunate in getting back again. The seas, I should judge, were running all of seventy feet high, and it would have made a landsman dizzy to have looked down into the trough. That was a boiling sea, and with all my going to sea I never saw its equal and hope I never shall again. After the large schooner passed us we did not see another sail until noon, when one appeared with hardly enough canvas spread to make an awning. We were seen from her and she began to drift towards us but missed us as another schooner ran between and by us.

The schooner was the Emily Northam, under command of Captain H. H. Stetson, as brave a captain as sails the

seas anywhere. When he found he was going to miss us he ran on out of sight, and very soon we saw him working back along towards us. My readers must understand that it took a smart man to keep his vessel afloat in that gale, to say nothing of working around to save the survivors from other vessels. My companions declared the schooner would not come back, but I was quite sure she would. Ned Walsh, one of the seamen, had dropped off and was floating with a piece of timber under each arm. The mate, R. S. Pettingill, was hanging to the forward part of the boat, and every sea that struck him knocked his breast against the boat.

I could see he was terribly hurt. The poor fellow, how I pitied him, and yet I could do nothing for him. I could see he was dying, and it was a terrible sight. His breast must have been crushed to a jelly, but he held on pluckily until just before the Emily Northam picked us up, when he dropped off. His body floated around and did not sink, so it was certain he was not drowned.

Kind friends, permit me to say there is not, I don't believe, one man in five hundred that could handle a vessel as Captain Stetson did that day, and as the story continues I will give my readers what Captain Stetson said about the rescue.

Charles Wickland, a Swede, the only seaman that was able to remain on the boat with me, was so overjoyed at the rescue that his mind was affected almost as soon as he got on board of the Northam, and had to be put into an asylum as soon as we arrived in port. My schooner was valued at four thousand dollars and was insured for twenty-five hundred dollars; the cargo was also valued at four thousand dollars.

Captain Stetson's home is in Revere, Mass., near Boston, and he is well known in this port, having sailed here for many years; he is a well-built man, with a clear blue eye and round, full face which shows nerve and firmness in every line. All of the shipping men who best understand and appreciate the bravery and skillful seamanship required in picking us up speak in high terms of him.

Captain Stetson says, in his modest way : " The storm as described by Captain Crapo was a fearful one, and we were fortunate as we did not lose a particle of canvas or part a rope. My wife and two children were on board at the time, a lass of thirteen and a lad of ten. After eating supper Tuesday night I went on deck and did not go below again until midday, Wednesday. The cook was bringing something on deck for the crew to eat, when the mate called out, ' There's a boat, Captain, with five people on it under our lee.' ' Take that back, cook; we have got to save those men before we eat,' I said. There was no way of getting to them except to drift, and that was attempted, and as we started the schooner scudded by us, between us and the boat, consequently the boat drifted by us. As I saw we had drifted by them I had all the sail put on I dared to and ran away from them, leaving them clinging to the boat.

"I ran out of sight, and I was afraid they would give up in despair. So as soon as I could I wore around and ran back. When I caught sight of them I began drifting. I intended to get them if it took all night, for I could not go and leave them to perish. It took me three hours, but at last I got headed so that I drifted right up to the man on the boards. As I came up the schooner laid over, her rail under water, and we picked him up, and as she righted he rolled in on deck, saved, thank God. Three minutes after I drifted down on the boat, and as it came alongside I reached my hand to Captain Crapo and pulled him on board.

" My wife gave the sailors some hot rum and they soon began to feel better. Captain Crapo refused to drink any. Wickland, the Swede, was so overjoyed at being rescued that his mind was affected almost as soon as he got on board my schooner, poor fellow ; yet situated as they were it is no wonder, as it takes nerves of steel to go through what they did alone on the mighty deep, clinging to a frail boat which was tumbled about like a chip by the mighty waves. Words cannot describe it, and it is a mystery how Captain Crapo ever got her in the water without her smashing to pieces.

" Captain Crapo says, in reply : ' When I saw that we would soon have to take to the boat, which was upside down on the forehatchway where she was lashed, I cut the lashings from her and rolled her over, and I began nailing strips of boards on the gunwale and put the oars in and lashed them amidships. I then nailed an awning around her which, with the oars, formed a sort of roof. I then ordered a keg of water put in and meat and provisions, as we did not know when we would be picked up, if at all. I then cut adrift two planks which were used to stay the deck load and lashed a line about eighty fathom long to them and threw them overboard, to act as a drogue for the boat. Several times while getting her ready heavy seas would board us and fill the boat nearly full of water. When we got all ready we had to work very careful in order to launch her safely, and we were very fortunate in doing so.' "

Our escape from a watery grave was indeed a miracle, and we are indebted to Captain Stetson for his timely assistance, as we could not have held on much longer, as we were very much exhausted. We were very thankful to be permitted to once more walk the deck of a good staunch vessel. Captain Stetson's destination was Savannah, Georgia, and as we had no choice of a landing place we were contented to proceed there with him. Everything that could be done for us was done by everyone on board, especially the captain, his wife and children, who seemed to be always looking for our comfort. Wickland, the sailor, was in a bad way, but with proper treatment in a quiet place he may regain his reason. At last we arrived at Savannah, and once more stepped on dry land, which was very pleasant to us after our terrible experience, and the news of our disaster spread like wildfire, and the evening paper called the Savannah Daily Times printed the following, which I will give just as it was printed :

SAVANNAH, GEORGIA, Monday, Aug. 31st, 1885.

FOUNDERED AT SEA.

Another victim of the hurricane of Tuesday last.—The schooner Gustie Wilson, from New York for Jacksonville, goes down off Cape Hatteras.—Her crew take to their boat.—Their fearful suffering.—Three drowned and three finally saved.

This morning the schooner Emily Northam, Captain H. H. Stetson, arrived in port, having been delayed on the way by the storm of Tuesday last. He reports that he had good weather until about fifty miles east of Hatteras, when a hurricane struck him with full force.

He hove his vessel to and made every preparation for meeting the storm, fortunately pulling through it all right, though badly shaken up. The next day about midday, while still hove to, a boat was sighted bottom up with three men clinging to it. He immediately prepared to go down to it and see what he could do towards rescuing the unfortunate sailors, but in this he had great difficulty as the wind was blowing terrible strong and the seas were rolling mountains high, and it was almost impossible to make any sail on the vessel. He, after three hours' hard work, managed to drift down to the boat, when he found that she belonged to the schooner Gustie Wilson, Captain Thomas Crapo, bound from New York to Jacksonville, Florida, with railroad iron. Every sea that hit the boat rolled her over and over, and washed those clinging to it for dear life as far as twenty feet away. They would swim back only to be washed off again. Captain Crapo estimates that this occurred at least one hundred times, but fortunately they were always enabled to regain the up-turned boat and keep themselves afloat.

At last they sighted the Northam and hope revived that they might be saved. After she had been sighted the mate died from exhaustion and floated away. Captain Crapo says, " We were on the bottom and clinging to the boat for six hours and carrying on a fearful battle for life."

There were six of us all told, but only three live to tell the tale, and they are badly used up. It was a terrible experience, and our escape from death was miraculous. They will always be able to relate a fearful tale of the sea, one of the most thrilling to which we have ever listened.

Captain Stetson further reports that he passed a great deal of wreckage all day yesterday, between St. Helena Sound and the lightship, consisting of boats, bales of goods, planks, drift-wood, and so on. The only thing he could pick up was a case of lard marked " Diamond G." He also passed a water tank and various other articles belonging to vessels. He is showing the rescued seamen every attention possible, and hopes to soon bring them around all right again. He says he cannot begin to express his feelings when he first saw them clinging to that capsized boat, especially when he found so much difficulty in getting to them, and when he got them on board he thinks he felt as happy as they did themselves.

According to the theory of Admiral Semmes we must have been caught in a cyclone. They are described as having two motions, one forward in the direction in which they are travelling, and another in a circle. Therefore when a vessel first encounters one of these dread disturbers of the elements, she is struck by the wind blowing in a certain direction. As the storm passes on its course the vessel gradually gets within the centre of the cyclone, and there is almost a dead calm.

As the storm continues on its courses the vessel encounters that portion of the circumference of the circle opposite to that which first struck her, and she finds herself again at the mercy of furious winds blowing from an entirely different direction. This was exactly the condition of the Wilson as described by Captain Crapo. She was struck on Friday night by the perimeter of the cyclonic circle, then the cyclone passed over her, and left her in a calm, then as it went on northward she was again struck by the circle, with the wind from an opposite direction, and she found it impossible to weather both attacks, consequently she foundered.

The Savannah Morning News of Feb. 15th, 1887, reads thus:

A Brave Man's Reward!

CAPTAIN STETSON'S HEROIC CONDUCT AT SEA WORTHILY RECOGNIZED.

About three weeks ago, just before leaving New York, Capt. H. H. Stetson, of the schooner Emily F. Northam, was presented with a handsome gold medal at the maritime exchange, by the Life Saving Humane Benevolent Society of New York, in recognition of his gallant rescue of Captain Crapo and two of his crew, of the wrecked schooner Gustie Wilson, August 26th, 1885. His act was applauded everywhere, and was considered a daring feat of seamanship in the way it was done. The captain is justly proud of his medal, and it is a just recognition of his gallant conduct.

After remaining in Savannah a few days I bid the Captain and his family good-bye, and proceeded to New York, having had a pass sent to me by the underwriters, and from there I returned to New Bedford, where I stayed quite a length of time, to recruit up.

Early the next spring I bought another schooner named the Oriole, and have followed the coasting business up to the present time. I am to-day in good health and spirits, and am at present only waiting for the spring to open, when I shall again bend sail and start in quest of cargoes, for one must be up and doing these days in order to keep their head above water.

I am in receipt of letters almost daily, with orders for photographs of my wife and myself, and many times of the boat, and as we get them by the thousand, we are always ready to meet the demand.

Hoping my efforts to please have been successful, I will close, with best wishes to all.

My late husband, Captain Crapo, bought the brig Manson of New Bedford in the spring of 1895. She was run very successfully in the coasting business, carrying lumber and general merchandise between Boston, Philadelphia and Norfolk, Va.—Captain Crapo being accompanied by myself on a good many of his voyages. It may be interesting to note here that I was always considered a fit first officer for the Manson, and it gives me all the more regret to speak of the loss of the brig, which occurred January 9th, 1898. In the beginning of January she left Norfolk, Va., with a cargo of lumber for Philadelphia, but encountered foggy weather, which became so severe that Captain Crapo deemed it advisable to make for Delaware breakwater, and in doing so the brig which he had made famous went ashore, and before assistance reached her there was no possible chance of saving her, on account of the severity of the storm. The tug North America was the one sent to her assistance, but before she reached the Manson the seas had played their sad havoc with the brig. I also desire to mention that with the famous Manson perished the still more famous 19-foot boat the New Bedford, on which Captain Crapo and myself crossed the Atlantic Ocean in 1877, which accomplishment is still fresh in the memory of the people.

A still greater loss has come to me since the loss of the Manson and the New Bedford, and it is this loss that has caused me to write this short article. While Captain Crapo was on his way from New Bedford to Cuba in a nine-foot boat named Volunteer this sad loss came to me. On his voyage he had visited Fall River, Providence,

Bristol and Newport. He left Newport May 3, 1899, and was never heard of again until his body was found off Charlestown beach, he having been drowned by the capsizing of his boat in a severe gale.

Just previous to the death of my husband he had the misfortune to lose almost his entire estate, on account of the loss of his vessel and other things, and I am now solely depending on the result of the book "Strange but True," published by my late husband and myself. I therefore commend the book to those who are in sympathy with increasing the sale of it, believing that it will be both entertaining and instructive to all who read it.

With my best wishes to all,

JOANNA CRAPO.

14 DAY USE
RETURN TO DESK FROM WHICH BORROWED

LOAN DEPT.

This book is due on the last date stamped below, or
on the date to which renewed.
Renewed books are subject to immediate recall.

23May'60C

REC'D LD

MAY 9 1960

2Feb'65

REC'D LD

JAN 19 '65 -8 PM

MAY 19 1969 4

MAY 5'69 -12 M

LOAN DEPT.

CPSIA information can be obtained
at www.ICGtesting.com
Printed in the USA
LVHW041020110319
610188LV00014B/272/P